ABIDING WORD

ABIDING WORD

SUNDAY REFLECTIONS FOR YEAR C

Barbara E. Reid, OP

LITURGICAL PRESS
Collegeville, Minnesota

www.litpress.org

2   3   4   5   6   7   8   9

Library of Congress Cataloging-in-Publication Data

Reid, Barbara E.
    Abiding word : Sunday reflections for year C / Barbara E. Reid.
       p.   cm.
    ISBN 978-0-8146-3313-7
    1. Church year meditations.   2. Bible—Meditations.   3. Catholic Church—Prayers and devotions.   4. Catholic Church. Lectionary for Mass (U.S.). Year C.   I. Title.

BX2170.C55R425   2012
242'.3—dc23   2012014726

CONTENTS

PREFACE

At the beginning of the Fourth Gospel, John the Baptist watches Jesus walk by and exclaims to two of his disciples, "Look, here is the Lamb of God!" (John 1:36). The two disciples begin to follow Jesus. When he turns and sees them following, he asks, "What are you looking for?" They reply, "Rabbi, where are you staying?" to which Jesus responds, "Come and see." So they do, and they remain with him that day (John 1:36-39). Staying, remaining, abiding (these are various ways that the Greek verb *menein* can be translated), is the primary response of a disciple. Different from the Synoptic Gospels, where disciples are more often seeking to understand who Jesus is, in the Fourth Gospel, the search is framed in terms of knowing where Jesus abides.

One of the key ways to abide in Jesus is through his word. Jesus tells those who believe in him, "If you continue in my word, you are truly my disciples, and you will know the truth, and the truth will make you free." Conversely, those who oppose him and look for an opportunity to kill him do so "because there is no place in you for my word" (John 8:31-38).

Another mode of abiding with Jesus is through Eucharist. After he feeds the multitude, Jesus tells his followers, "Those who eat my flesh and drink my blood abide in me and I in them" (John 6:56). This mutual indwelling, we in Christ and Christ in us, is deepened each Sunday through the word and at the table.

I offer this collection of reflections on the Scripture readings for each Sunday and solemnity for the Lectionary Year C as a weekly aid to enter more deeply into the abiding word, and to enable a renewed response to remain with Jesus. These reflections first appeared in *America* magazine, from November 23, 2009 to November 15, 2010 (vol. 201, no. 16–vol. 203, no. 14), and have been slightly edited for this volume.

I invite you to establish a pattern of dwelling with the word each day, if possible. Some suggestions for how to approach the word follow. Many find it helpful to set aside the same block of time each day, and to sit in one particular place, in a chapel, or in a favorite easy chair, claiming this as your sacred time and sacred space. Sit with your spine straight, feet flat on the floor, and concentrate on your breathing. As you breathe in, and breathe out, invite the Spirit, whom Jesus promised will abide with us always (John 14:17), to open your mind, eyes, ears, and heart to the word that the Holy One wants to give you this day. Consciously set aside all other concerns, distractions, and worries. Imagine leaving them outside the door of your holy space. If they try to intrude into your prayer, tell them they have to wait until you have finished, and that you will pick them up again later.

Open the Scriptures and read the text slowly and contemplatively. Savor each word and phrase. Imagine yourself as one of the characters in the story if the text is a narrative. What do you see? hear? smell? feel? Read through the text again slowly and prayerfully. Is there a particular word or phrase that catches your attention? Stay with that word or phrase and let it take deeper root in you. Wait patiently for whatever it is that is being revealed to you in that word. Even if there is no clear insight or special meaning that emerges, trust that the word is abiding in you and unleashing its trans-formative power in you. Let yourself be led to see differently, for example, from the perspective of those made poor, of women, or of those not like yourself. Set aside what you "know" the text means and let yourself be surprised by the Spirit. Respond with thanks for what has been given to you by the abiding One. Hold on to a word or phrase from the Scripture and return to it throughout the day. Jot it down in your prayer journal, so you can return to it at another time. Let its meaning continue to unfold as you abide in it and it in you.

In the Gospel of John, as Jesus approaches his death, he tells his disciples that he prepares a dwelling place for each one, so that where he is they may also be. Thomas struggles, insisting he does not know the way. Jesus assures him that Jesus himself is the way, the truth, and the life. The abiding place, then, is not a special "room with a view," so to speak, but is Jesus himself. Abiding in Jesus leads also to indwelling with the One who sent him and with the Spirit, as Jesus prayed for oneness, "I in them" and "they in us" and "I in them" and "you in me" (John 17:20-23).

The gift of abiding in Christ and Christ in the believer is a priceless trea-sure meant not only for oneself. It is a fruitful gift, one that is intended to be shared with others, producing a harvest of transformative love (John 15:1-8).

Barbara E. Reid, OP
Feast of the Presentation of the Lord, 2012

PROMISES FULFILLED

First Sunday of Advent

Readings: Jer 33:14-16; Ps 25:4-5, 8-9, 10, 14;
1 Thess 3:12–4:2; Luke 21:25-28, 34-36

"Beware that your hearts do not become drowsy" (Luke 21:34)

How do people who fall in love sustain their hopeful expectation of one another throughout their lives? Some relationships begin to crumble after the infatuation wears off, the delight in mutual commitment fades, and routine life settles in. Some relationships don't make it through a lifetime. Others weather the passage of time with moments of renewed celebration of promises made and kept, and of crises faced together, strengthening the lifelong bond. Such experiences in human relationships reveal something of how God interacts with us.

As Advent begins, people in the Northern Hemisphere may be inclined to snuggle into the shortened dark days of approaching winter to calmly contemplate the coming of Christ. But the readings put us in a crisis-mode that is anything but restful. Jeremiah addresses the exiles who are undergoing great distress. He had earlier prophesied that the Davidic dynasty would be restored soon after the fall of Jerusalem. Instead, the weary exiles have experienced disaster after disaster, and they are grasping for some sign of hope. "The days are coming" is an expression that in the Bible ordinarily introduces a pronouncement of judgment, instilling fear in the hearers. Instead, Jeremiah uses the phrase to startle the careworn exiles with an assurance that God will fulfill the promises made to Israel and Judah.

As partners whose relationship has hit the rocks may be able to recapture the initial fervor of their love when reminded of the joy and delight with which their promises of commitment were made, so God's beloved are wooed away from their woes to focus on the sure promise of redemption at hand. There is a wordplay: Israel's last king was Zedekiah, whose name derives from the Hebrew word for "justice." While the people look for a new "just shoot" from David's branch, Jeremiah proclaims that it is God's own self who is "our justice."

While Jeremiah's hearers were waiting for fulfillment of God's promises in an existing crisis, Luke and Paul's hearers are waiting for an apocalyptic end time that seems long in coming. Luke's warning is not to let one's heart grow drowsy during the long wait. Like lovers whose passion fades and whose lives are lulled into routine, the people's ardor may dim and they may be found unprepared for the coming crisis. Luke advises not letting our hearts go after things that satisfy only for a time, and not becoming weighed down with anxiety. Be always watchful, he says, so as not to be taken by surprise. Pray for strength, and do not be at all afraid. Stand tall, he says, raise your heads, and be ready for the embrace of the One who is Love Incarnate.

Paul tells the Thessalonians to strengthen their hearts. He prays, "May the Lord make you increase and abound in love for one another and for all," reminding us that it is God who initiates and sustains us in love, and that it is a love meant to be shared with all. Daily prayer and practices of loving outreach prepare us well for the crisis times, when disaster strikes, when jobs are lost, when illness or death turns our world awry, when violence rips at the fabric of our world. With hearts already strengthened by God's love, we are able to withstand any assault.

The expectation of the birth of a child can often reignite the ardor of a flagging love relationship. So too in Advent, if our hearts are weary or drowsy, our preparation for the celebration of the Christ, who has already been born as one of us, can spark our love once again, not only toward the One who came as a child in our midst, but also to all God's beloved children.

PRAYING WITH SCRIPTURE

1. How are you keeping your heart from becoming drowsy this Advent?

2. How has God strengthened your heart in times of crisis?

3. How have you experienced the God who fulfills promises?

ROUGH WAYS MADE SMOOTH

Second Sunday of Advent

Readings: Bar 5:1-9;
Ps 126:1-2, 2-3, 4-5, 6; Phil 1:4-6, 8-11; Luke 3:1-6

"The Lord has done great things for us; we are filled with joy" (Ps 126:3)

In some cultures, a woman who has been widowed or who loses a child wears black for a year or more, signaling her mourning. Her face too wears the marks of grief. The sparkle in her eyes gives way to ready tears and her gait becomes heavy from sorrow. Such is the image of the city of Jerusalem in today's first reading.

Baruch, a disciple of Jeremiah, characterizes the devastated city as a woman in mourning for her exiled children who have been forcibly taken away from her. The prophet declares that it is now time for Jerusalem to exchange her robe of mourning and misery for a brilliant new mantle. Her new cloak is spun from justice and glory from God. If she despaired for her children, thinking God had forgotten them, the prophet insists that "they are remembered by God."

The humiliation of their forced march into exile on foot will be undone by their being carried back aloft, as if they were royalty. The heights of despair and the depths of depression will be leveled out. It is not that the suffering is forgotten, or that anything could go back to being the way it was before the tragedy, but now the divine gift of joy settles over the grieving mother as rebuilding life out of the ruins begins. The returnees are led by God's light, and their companions are mercy and justice.

Divine mercy embodies God's motherly care, as she grieves with all who mourn and acts with compassion to bring relief for all who suffer. Divine justice is the setting aright of all relationships: with God, self, others, and the whole of the cosmos. With these two companions come healing, restoration, and the chance for a new beginning.

In the gospel, there is a similar invitation to a new beginning announced by John the Baptist. The narrative starts on an ominous note, as John's ministry is set against the backdrop of the Roman imperial rulers. Luke is not simply displaying an interest in history by naming Tiberius Caesar, the emperor; Pontius Pilate, the governor; Herod, Philip, and Lysanias, the tetrarchs; and finally, Annas and Caiaphas, the high priests who colluded with the Roman authorities. He is reminding his hearers of the omnipresent imperial power that kept the inhabitants of Palestine in fear and grief at many levels. He foreshadows the terror of John's execution and of Jesus' crucifixion by introducing Herod and Pilate before these two prophets have even spoken their opening words.

Luke's hearers already know the end of the story. It is in this context that we hear John's invitation not only to turn away from personal choices that impede God's coming but also to collective repentance and a turn toward divine mercy. Any desire for revenge, any attempts to try to retaliate with violence, must give way to forgiveness on the part of the victims. This forgiveness invites repentance on the part of the offenders. Using Isaiah's words, John first speaks in imperatives: prepare and make straight the way. But then the verbs shift to the passive voice, implying that it will be the Coming One himself who will do the filling in of the valleys and leveling of the mountains, straightening out winding roads, and smoothing the rough ways.

For them and for us, his coming does not eliminate these challenges along life's path but fills us with saving joy, justice, forgiveness, and mercy as we open ourselves to the great things God has done and continues to do for us.

PRAYING WITH SCRIPTURE

1. What robe of mourning does God wish to take away from you in order to clothe you with joy and splendor?

2. How has God's compassion carried you over the rough places of your journey?

3. What is being healed, forgiven, and restored in you as you prepare the way this Advent?

GOD'S JOY

Third Sunday of Advent

Readings: Zeph 3:14-18a;
Isa 12:2-3, 4, 5-6; Phil 4:4-7; Luke 3:10-18

"The crowds asked John the Baptist, 'What should we do?'" (Luke 3:10)

"You will know." This was the sage advice I received from a wise mentor at a time when I was at a crossroads in making an important life decision. How much easier it would be, I thought, if someone could just tell me what was the right thing to do. I knew, however, that my mentor was right. No one else could answer the deepest questions for me about the choice to be made. She pointed me to the heart of wisdom residing within me, by which I would know what was the Spirit's prompting.

In today's gospel, one group after another wants John the Baptist to help them know what they should do. They have been touched by his invitation to repent and believe the good news and have been washed free of all their sinful choices from the past. But what's the next step? There is no one-size-fits-all response. John's advice is tailored to each according to his or her circumstances. Nothing he suggests is very dramatic or extraordinary: If you have extra clothing, then share it with those who have none. If you have food, then share it with those who are hungry. If you collect money, take only what you need. And if you have military might, do not abuse it. These admonitions seem obvious—they are things that "you will know" if you listen to the wisdom within. When Zephaniah declares, "God is in your midst," it is a reassurance that the divine guidance resides within each person and within each believing community when they allow their hearts to be turned toward the Holy One. The freedom and joy that well up from accepting God's forgiving love is, as Isaiah says in the responsorial psalm, like drawing water at a fountain of salvation. You can return to this fountain again and again to drink deeply of its saving power. A fountain circulates living, active water, always fresh and pure, not like a cistern that collects "dead" water in a stagnant pool. At the fountain of salvation one drinks in joy, courage, and strength, which overflow in our actions toward others.

The theme of joy weaves throughout the readings and the liturgy on this Gaudete (Latin for "rejoice") Sunday. The joy is not only our own, from the forgiveness and salvation that set us free, but God also rejoices and sings, delighting in renewing us in love (Zeph 3:17-18). This joy and mutual delight want to be shared in wider and wider circles. What shall we do to make that happen? You will know.

In the gospel John the Baptist speaks about a more advanced stage of turning toward God. Beyond the baptism of repentance and its freeing joy is a further "baptism" with "the Holy Spirit and fire" that the Christ brings. Followers of Jesus will be empowered by the Spirit, who emboldens them for all manner of ministries. They will also undergo a purification process, a winnowing away of any imperfections that impede God's love and joy. The winnowing is not so much a process that separates out people who tend to do good and people who tend more to sin; rather, it is a refining for all who turn to Christ, a burning away of all that keeps us from experiencing God's delight and from knowing how to share that with others. This, then, is what distinguishes joy from optimism. A cheery outlook is not necessarily a Christian virtue. But a radical joy that accompanies a refinement by fire is one of the paradoxical hallmarks of our faith.

PRAYING WITH SCRIPTURE

1. Sit with God and feel the joy of the Holy One who delights over you.

2. How do you answer the question, "What should we do?"

3. How has your joy grown through experiences of purifying "fire"?

LEAPING FOR JOY

Fourth Sunday of Advent

Readings: Mic 5:1-4a;
Ps 80:2-3, 15-16, 18-19; Heb 10:5-10; Luke 1:39-45

*"For at the moment the sound of your greeting reached my ears,
the infant in my womb leaped for joy"* (Luke 1:44)

There are certain persons in our lives who, when we see them or hear their voices, make our hearts skip a beat with delight. They are the ones who can make us laugh when everything seems gray. They are the ones who have strong arms and soft hearts, who wrap us in a smothering bear hug that makes everything seem alright. They are the wise ones who have weathered many a storm and whose assurances that all will be well can be trusted absolutely. Such is the meeting of Mary and Elizabeth in today's gospel. The moment Elizabeth heard Mary's voice, both her own heart and the babe in her womb leaped for joy. Mary undoubtedly felt the same.

Oftentimes we imagine Mary, the younger of the two, hastening from Galilee to Judea out of concern and generosity to help her older relative, who is coping with pregnancy at an advanced age. Without discounting this aspect of their encounter, we may also envision Elizabeth as the wise figure of an elder mentor, who wraps the bewildered teenage mother-to-be in her strong embrace, offering her wisdom and strength in a difficult time. God's timing is difficult for both women. How much easier it would have been for Elizabeth had her child come when her body was more limber and supple. How much easier it would have been for Mary had her child arrived after her marriage to Joseph.

In a culture in which a woman was esteemed for the male children she bore, Elizabeth likely endured accusatory glances and unkind comments throughout her life as people wondered why God was punishing her with barrenness. Likewise, in Mary's little village, Nazareth, the gossip about her probably started flying once her condition was known. Elizabeth, who has been utterly faithful to God all her life long (Luke 1:6), despite the suffering she has endured, is the perfect companion for Mary. She helps Mary learn to trust even more deeply the mysterious ways of God as she endures the many difficulties that come with saying yes to God.

In like manner, we too carry the mysterious power of God's life within us, which enables us to be a source of delight and blessing for others. When we abandon ourselves to the mysterious ways of God, it is not only for ourselves that the new life within is given. We are meant to be companions to one another, a source of mutual joy, wisdom, and strength.

PRAYING WITH SCRIPTURE

1. Give thanks to God for those who make your heart leap for joy this Advent.

2. Ask for the grace to let the sound of your voice be a source of delight for others.

IN GOD'S BOSOM

The Nativity of the Lord

Readings: Isa 52:7-10;
Ps 98:1, 2-3, 3-4, 5-6; Heb 1:1-6; John 1:1-18

"It is God the only son, who is close to the Father's heart,
who has made him known" (John 1:18, NRSV)

No one has ever seen God—or so the ancients said. They believed you could not see God because God was invisible. Or, if one did see God, that person would not live to tell of it. Thus, Moses asks to see God's glory, not God's face. He is protected in a cleft of a rock, and covered by God's hand when God passes by. He is allowed to see God's back, as God tells him, "you cannot see my face; for no one shall see me and live" (Exod 33:20, NRSV).

In the same way, today's gospel affirms, "we saw his glory"—but even more, divinity has become entirely visible in the Word made flesh. In the face of Jesus and in the face of all his followers, we see God's face—and live to tell of it! The exquisite poetry of John's prologue takes us back to the origins of the cosmos, to the explosion of light and heat when life came into existence, brought into being by the power of God and the Word, one in being, one in generative love.

This divine desire to share love and life culminates with the "pitching of a tent" by the Word among humankind. In the desert sojourn with Israel, God would speak with Moses in the tent of meeting that Moses set up outside the camp. A pillar of cloud would descend upon it when Moses entered it to speak with God; then Moses would return to the camp (Exod 33:7-11). With the birth of Jesus, God inhabits the "tent" of human flesh, not in a place apart, but right in our midst.

Whereas Moses entered the tent for a solitary encounter with God, now God enters the tent of humanity so as to make "grace upon grace" directly available to every single one. This divine love and intimacy are revealed to us by the "only Son" who is "in the bosom of the Father."

The intimacy of this relationship is not always as vividly expressed, as some translations render this phrase in John 1:18 as "at the Father's side."

A more literal translation is "in the bosom" (*kolpos*) or "breast" of the Father. This image is reprised in John 13:23, when, at the Last Supper, the Beloved Disciple is reclining "in the bosom [*kolpos*] of Jesus" (my translation). The same intimacy between the Father and Jesus is shared with all disciples, who make visible in every generation the face of God in human flesh.

PRAYING WITH SCRIPTURE

1. Whose face most clearly revealed God to you today?

2. What does it feel like to be in the bosom of God?

GOD'S FAMILY REUNION

"Did you not know that I must be in my Father's house?" (Luke 2:49)

It was the empty place at the table that sounded the alarm for the worried parents. After a day's travel, enjoying the camaraderie of the extended family, the nightly meal revealed that their son was missing. The circumstances may be different, but most families know what it is to have an empty place at the table—a place meant for a son or daughter who is absent because of estrangement or because other duties have taken precedence or death has claimed them too early. During the rest of the day, the family may manage without the absent one, but it is the gaping hole at the table that is the hardest to endure. Sometimes the story ends happily. The soldier returns home in time for the next holiday; a sick child recovers; an alienated member becomes reconciled; a missing teen is found unscathed.

In the gospel today, there is at first a note of relief that Jesus is found unharmed. But a more ominous note sounds when Jesus declares he must be in his Father's house. We already know the end of the story. We know that as Jesus builds a new family to abide in his Father's house, he will offend some religious leaders by filling in the empty places at the table with people whom others did not consider part of the family. Jesus claimed that all these unwanted folk were God's beloved children.

The gospel episode ends with Jesus returning to Nazareth with Mary and Joseph, saying that he "was obedient to them" and that he "advanced in wisdom and age and favor." We sometimes imagine Jesus as a reluctant teen, who has to continue to abide by his earthly parents' rules, even as he feels he must begin to pursue his life's work in response to God's call. Throughout his opening chapters, however, Luke has portrayed Jesus'

earthly parents as utterly law-observant and completely conforming themselves to God's will.

There is no tension between what God asks and what they choose to do.
Mary assents to Gabriel, even though she does not understand everything
that is asked of her. Mary and Joseph obediently have their child circumcised after eight days, and then present him in the temple in Jerusalem, as
the law prescribes. Every year, they go to Jerusalem for the feast of Passover. We might see, then, in the ending of today's gospel, that there is no
conflict between Jesus' obedience to Mary and Joseph and his obedience
to the will of God. Rather, it is Mary and Joseph who have taught Jesus
how to recognize the call of God and how to be obedient to it. It is in their
home in Nazareth that he will continue to grow in wisdom and grace and
in the ability to discern what is obedience to God. It is through his earthly
parents that Jesus will come to understand how precious and beloved he
is as God's Chosen One. It is from listening to his mother's song, which
dreams of the hungry being well fed and the lowly lifted up, that Jesus
learns obedience to God's inclusive love. We too learn in our homes that
we are already God's beloved children, as the reading from 1 John asserts.
It is not a privilege to be earned but a gift already bestowed. And just as
Hannah longed fervently for Samuel, so God longs to dandle each of us on
her knees and wrap us in her loving arms. We already have a place at the
table in God's family and are invited to remain there.

As the second reading reminds us, we make the family resemblance visible in our shared belief in the Son and in our obedience to the command to
love one another. When we gather as church, as God's family, we find healing and forgiveness from all that is not perfect in our birth families. There
are no empty places at the table of God's family reunions, where all the lost
come home and grow in wisdom through obedience to the Source of Love.

PRAYING WITH SCRIPTURE

1. Pray for the grace to treasure in your heart, as Mary did, the ways of
God that are not immediately understood.

2. Give thanks for all the siblings who sit with us at God's family table.

NAMED FOR JESUS

**The Blessed Virgin Mary,
Mother of God**

Readings: Num 6:22-27;
Ps 67:2-3, 5, 6, 8; Gal 4:4-7; Luke 2:16-21

*"So shall they invoke my name upon the Israelites,
and I will bless them"* (Num 6:27)

As a child, I did not understand my grandfather's consternation that he did not have a son who would carry on his name. It was clear that he was enormously proud of his three daughters and that he loved them with all his heart. But each of them took her husband's name in marriage and none would pass on his surname. I remember his utter delight when my brother was born and my parents gave him my grandfather's first name.

In the Bible, bestowing a name is a critically important act. Naming is a way of identifying relationship, as the first human does when God presents the animals to him to see what he will call them (Gen 2:19). Often a name reflects something of the nature of the person, as when Adam calls the first woman "Eve, because she was the mother of all the living" (Gen 3:20, NABRE). Sometimes the name expresses the parents' experience of God, as when Hannah names her son Samuel, explaining, "I have asked him of the LORD" (1 Sam 1:20, NRSV). Just so, Elizabeth and Zechariah name their son "John," "God is gracious," or "gift of God," since they know it is not by human means alone that this child was conceived. Mary and Joseph call their son Jesus, whose name evokes the Hebrew expression "God saves" (see Matt 1:21), expressing their longing for a new experience of God's freeing power for themselves and their people from all that holds them bound.

There is a power in naming. The Navajo have a saying that if you name a thing, it becomes. This is illustrated in a scene in the novel *The Help* by Kathryn Stockett (New York: Penguin, 2009). A little girl whose mother has no time for her and who only scolds her for her shortcomings is cared for tenderly by her maid, who takes her face in her hands and tells her repeatedly, "You is kind,

13

you is smart, you is important." As the baby girl repeats these words after Aibileen, one can see her believing and becoming what she is being named.

A thread that runs through each of today's readings is the naming of us as God's own children, calling us forth to become heirs of the divine promise. When Moses tells the Israelites that God's name is put upon them, they not only experience God's blessing, graciousness, and peace, but themselves become a source of those divine gifts for others.Paul, in writing to the Galatians, emphasizes their status as God's children. Adopted by God, they bear the divine name; they are heirs to everything that is God's. They will never bear anyone else's name or belong as slaves to anyone else again.

On this day when we pray for world peace, the readings invite Jesus' followers to claim our inheritance from the One after whom we are named. As well, they ask us to hold in our embrace all our sisters and brothers, each person and creature on the planet, all named after our same divine parent, all full heirs to our shared inheritance.

PRAYING WITH SCRIPTURE

1. How do you live the inheritance given by your Divine Parent for whom you have been named?

2. How do you name others as beloved children of God?

3. How does naming enable something to become?

WISDOM'S RESTING PLACE

Second Sunday after Christmas

Readings: Sir 24:1-2, 8-12;
Ps 147:12-13, 14-15, 19-20; Eph 1:3-6, 15-18; John 1:1-18

"Among all these I sought a resting place" (Sir 24:7, NABRE)

Just when we think we may have been challenged enough, trying to grasp the unfathomable mystery of God become flesh, the very same gospel we pondered on Christmas Day comes back to us, this time paired with a hymn to Wisdom from Sirach 24. The echoes between the two readings are unmistakable. Just as Wisdom tells of her glory, so the glory of the Word is seen in the incarnation. Just as Wisdom dwelt in the highest heavens and was then given a command to make her dwelling place with Israel, so the Word dwelt with God before coming to tent among humankind. Wisdom was created before the ages and shall not cease to be, just as the Word was with God in the beginning, and will exist forever. If it is difficult to embrace the mystery of God taking on human flesh in Christ, we are now invited to stretch our imaginations all the more, to see the divine made manifest in female form.

In addition to Sirach 24, the texts in the Old Testament that feature Woman Wisdom (Job 28; Prov 1–9; Bar 3:9–4:4; Sir 1; 4:11-19; 6:18-31; 14:20-15; Wis 6–10) do not speak of wisdom as an attribute of God but as a personification of the very being of God. Just as the Word is the divine made wholly manifest in human flesh in male form, so Wisdom is the embodiment of the divine made manifest in female form. Our belief in the Word having taken up his abode in human flesh invites us to see the divine in all persons. Wisdom, who likewise has found her resting place in God's people, opens the horizon for us to see the divine fully manifest in female persons and images as well as male.

In three places in today's gospel, the Fourth Evangelist helps us to stretch our imaginations beyond the edges of gender boundaries. First, the author speaks of the Logos, the Word, who we come to understand as Jesus, as giving birth to all things that came to be (v. 3). Then, God is said to give birth to children through faith in the Logos (v. 13). And in the final verse of the prologue, the evangelist asserts that the Son is ever at the bosom of the Father (v. 18), melding the image of Father with that of a nursing mother. Later, Jesus uses the imagery of being born again/from above (there is a wordplay in Greek) when speaking with Nicodemus about entering the reign of God (3:3-7). And in the last discourse, he describes his coming passion as birth pangs that give way to joy when new life is born (16:20-22).

The blurring of gender in the Fourth Gospel coupled with the texts where Woman Wisdom embodies the divine aids us in being able to perceive God made manifest in women's experience, in female form, and in women's bodies. To come to full acceptance of God being equally revealed in female form as in male and of the risen Christ transcending gender is as difficult a journey as the first Christians experienced when they struggled over the boundaries between Jew and Gentile, slave and free. As Paul prays in today's second reading for the Ephesians, so too he prays with and for us, that we may receive a spirit of wisdom, and that the eyes of our hearts be enlightened, as we dwell in this great mystery.

PRAYING WITH SCRIPTURE

1. How is Holy Wisdom inviting you into a deeper understanding of God?

2. Invite Wisdom to make her dwelling place in you.

3. Rest with the Son in the bosom of the Father.

THE HIDDEN REVEALED

The Epiphany of the Lord

Readings: Isa 60:1-6; Ps 72:1-2, 7-8,
10-11, 12-13; Eph 3:2-3a, 5-6; Matt 2:1-12

"[T]he mystery was made known to me by revelation" (Eph 3:3)

A favorite game of children of all ages is hide-and-seek. There is a certain thrill in thinking that one can become momentarily invisible to the seeker. Then come the peals of delight and surprise when the hiding place is discovered and once again one's whereabouts are clearly known. Today's feast centers on the hiddenness of God's plan having been revealed to all, without discrimination. For Jew and Gentile alike, God's love bursts forth like a light that pierces the darkness, like a child's squeals of delight when found. There is no hiding from this wondrous gift as it reaches to the ends of the earth.

There is a tradition in Latin America and in Hispanic communities in the United States that on El Día de los Reyes, the "Day of the Kings," a small plastic baby Jesus is hidden in a cake baked specially for the feast day. The figurine is nestled within the dough, signifying the efforts to hide the child Jesus from the evil intentions of King Herod. As the cake is cut, the slicing knife represents the danger posed to the infant Jesus by the cruel king.

In some places the tradition is that whoever gets the piece of cake with the figurine is obliged to host the next family gathering on February 2, the feast of the Presentation. In other places, the one who finds the baby Jesus in his or her portion receives an array of gifts from those present. These traditions make tangible both the danger inherent in the revelation of the Christ and the excitement of the hidden designs of God become manifest.

In the gospel, the danger is most palpable as the exotic visitors from the East wisely discern the true king who has been revealed, in contrast to Rome's puppet king, who wants to engage in a sinister version of hide-and-seek. Herod tries to get the magi to "search diligently for the child" and then bring Herod word when they find him. But the plan is foiled when a divine warning in a dream directs the magi to return to their country by another way.

These visitors from an unknown land also cause us to reflect on the gifts that come to us in hidden ways from those we regard as strangers. Their odd dress, differently colored skin, and unintelligible tongue immediately put us on guard.

Those who are different are often a source of fear for us, but in today's gospel, they are friends, coheirs to the promise, and the first to recognize the hidden plans of God. In the gospel narrative, these extraordinary visitors appear only briefly. Would we welcome such strangers who reveal the hidden Holy One in our midst if they were to stay?

PRAYING WITH SCRIPTURE

1. What hidden mystery about the Christ is being revealed in you?

2. How have the gifts of strangers revealed Christ to you?

LOVE ENOUGH FOR ALL

The Baptism of the Lord

Readings: Isa 42:1-4, 6-7;
Ps 29:1-2, 3-4, 3, 9-10; Acts 10:34-38; Luke 3:15-16, 21-22

"In truth, I see that God shows no partiality" (Acts 10:34)

Ask any parent which of their children they love the most, and typically the response will be "I love all my children equally." Ask any child and you will hear otherwise. The oldest daughter thinks she is favored as firstborn and that she holds prime place in her mother's affections. The youngest son thinks he is the apple of his father's eye. The middle child knows her specialness—how could she not be the most beloved?

In the second reading today we see Peter as a kind of older sibling, wrestling to let go of his notion that, as one who belongs to God's firstborn, he could claim primacy of affection from his heavenly parent. The scene in Acts 10 is the culmination of a very difficult struggle on Peter's part to accept the fact that God's favor could also include others who were not part of God's firstborn. It took a thrice-repeated vision before Peter could recognize Cornelius as one of God's favored. Peter's initial opposition to the heavenly voice that instructed him to eat something he considered unclean was emphatic (vv. 13-14): "Certainly not" (NABRE); "By no means" (NRSV).

After entering Cornelius's house, Peter conversed with the centurion (v. 27). Undoubtedly, in the course of their exchange, Peter discovers that he is not the only one to whom God has spoken through visions. Cornelius too has encountered an angel of God who has called him by name (v. 3). Moreover, Peter finds that this man prays constantly and gives alms generously (v. 2). Peter has to admit to all in the house that whoever fears God and acts uprightly is "acceptable" to God. He acknowledges that "God shows no partiality."

While this is a great breakthrough for Peter, his recognition of Cornelius as "acceptable" is not exactly a ringing endorsement. Might there be a hint in Peter's statement that he still considers himself among "God's favorites," and that he thinks of Cornelius more like a stepbrother who certainly could not displace him in the divine affections? More time would be needed before Peter could see the Gentile as being loved as passionately by God as himself.

In the gospel another heavenly revelation highlights Jesus' specialness as God's beloved. While the divine voice at Jesus' baptism is directed to him ("You are my beloved Son"; cf. Matt 3:17, "This is my beloved Son"), Luke has added "all the people" to the scene. In this way, Luke hints that they too experience the delight of God in them, as they are washed clean, newly born, and favored. As we recall our own baptism, we know that we too have been in that thin space where "heaven was opened" and the barrier between humanity and divinity is dissolved. With Jesus taking on human flesh, and then inviting us to partake of his flesh and blood, the special place he holds in God's affection is extended to all.

That God is partial to each of us is something startling. This divine favor causes wonder and also carries with it a mission. In the first reading, Isaiah elaborates the mission entrusted to a chosen servant: to bring forth justice. In biblical parlance, justice does not mean that everyone gets what he or she deserves. Rather, it signifies that those who know themselves to be favored by God undeservedly have been empowered by the Spirit to be light, to speak truth, and to be compassionate to those who feel like "a bruised reed," fanning into flame the spark of God's love wherever a smoldering wick is found.

PRAYING WITH SCRIPTURE

1. Reflect on how God has shown partiality toward you.

2. How does that divine favor move you to work for justice?

OUT OF THE WILDERNESS

First Sunday of Lent

Readings: Deut 26:4-10; Ps 91:1-2, 10-11,
12-13, 14-15; Rom 10:8-13; Luke 4:1-13

"You shall not put the Lord, your God, to the test" (Luke 4:13)

"Where is God?" was the refrain posed by a sister who ministers in Port au Prince as she recounted to a group of religious leaders stories of immense suffering and death following the earthquake in Haiti. Was God in the earthquake? Did God send it to test our faith? How can we recognize the voice of a loving God in such times of desolation?

Today's gospel shows Jesus in a similar time of struggle. He is returning from the Jordan, where he has just been baptized by John, a powerful experience of knowing the certainty of God's delight in him as beloved Son. He has also sensed the Spirit making a home in him. The contrast between this idyllic scene at the river and his bleak struggle in the desert is stark. Doubts come flooding over Jesus: Was that experience in the Jordan to be trusted? Is he truly loved by God? If God is so loving, then why do people go hungry? Why does the all-powerful One let the rulers of the world grab power and glory for themselves instead of looking out for the good of their people? Why doesn't God save beloved ones from disaster? At stake in this struggle is the question of both who is God and who is Jesus as beloved Son of God. *"If you* are the Son of God . . ." taunts the tempter. And so it is with us too, when great trials shake our self-understanding and cause us to question our reliance on God.

The readings today do not provide reasoned arguments in answer to these deep questions, but they do show us a way to engage the struggles as we are invited more deeply into the mystery of suffering, dying, and rising as God's cherished ones. The reading from Deuteronomy reminds us of the long history of God's saving deeds and asks us to declare these, to remind us that our faith in times of trouble is not baseless.

In the gospel, we see Jesus relying on the word of God to guide and strengthen him. He engages in a kind of Bible battle with the devil, a sobering reminder that anyone can quote Scripture to his or her own purposes. Jesus shows that daily immersion of ourselves in Scripture enables us to recognize the authentic voice of God and reject the traitorous lead of the tempter. Jesus unmasks the false allure of believing in a God who would prove divine love by acting like an indulgent parent, giving in to our every desire. He exposes the untruth of believing in a God whose power is displayed in ostentatious empires, or in manipulating the laws of nature. His replies to the devil reveal that God does not send misfortune to test us, nor does God respond to "tests" that we construct in order to prove God's loving nature. God is not a sadistic puppeteer, who dallies with us to see whether we will keep steady in our faith. God is continually drawing us ever more deeply into the mystery of the divine love, most especially in times of greatest adversity.

Lent provides us an opportunity to embrace anew such struggles as Jesus faced. Like him, we claim the power of the Spirit that has been given to us in baptism, and daily immerse ourselves in the word, which, as Paul reminds, is ever near, in our mouth and in our heart. Clarity in hearing that word comes when we go apart to deserted spaces, and when we fast so as to sharpen our hunger for God and for acting in solidarity with God's starving people. Such practices prepare us to find God in the faces of those who suffer, and to be ready for the final struggle, where like Jesus we readily pray, "into your hands I commend my spirit" (Luke 23:46; Ps 31:6, NABRE).

PRAYING WITH SCRIPTURE

1. What favorite Scripture passage do you keep "in your mouth and in your heart"?

2. How have times of great adversity drawn you more deeply into the mystery of God's love?

3. What Lenten practices help you respond more intently to God's word?

THE FACE OF FREEDOM

Second Sunday of Lent

Readings: Gen 15:5-12, 17-18; Ps 27:1, 7-8, 8-9, 13-14; Phil 3:17–4:1; Luke 9:28-36

"While he was praying his face changed in appearance" (Luke 9:29)

A missionary friend working in a country where many forms of violence are a part of the fabric of everyday life remarked to me recently that she is very conscious that she can choose whether to stay or leave. This is a choice that the people to whom she has dedicated her life do not have. Some friends and family members do not understand how she could choose to put her own life in danger for the sake of the people she has come to love as her own.

Such a choice faces Jesus in today's gospel. In Luke's version of this story, which we hear every year on the Second Sunday of Lent, there are unique details that point to an earlier source that tell us more clearly what really happened at the transfiguration.

The episode is set at an important turning point in the gospel. Jesus has been teaching, preaching, healing, exorcising demons, and gathering disciples as he traverses the Galilee. But soon he will "set his face to go to Jerusalem" (9:51, NRSV). Something happens on the mountaintop that helps Jesus to know what is his next step in his mission. Luke alone notes that when Jesus goes up the mountain with Peter, James, and John, his purpose is to pray.

A clue to the nature of Jesus' prayer comes in the content of the conversation between Jesus, Moses, and Elijah. They "spoke of his exodus that he was going to accomplish in Jerusalem." Jesus is wrestling with the decision whether he should leave the Galilee and direct his efforts toward Jerusalem, the center of religious and political power. There is still much to do in the Galilee, and he could continue to minister there, but he struggles to know whether his efforts could bring about greater systemic change if he were to go to Jerusalem.

But Jesus is no fool. The handwriting is on the wall. Opposition to him is already mounting, and it would only intensify if he were to go to Jerusalem. As at every major turning point in the gospel, Jesus enters into deep communion with God as he discerns what to do.

In this profound encounter with God, Jesus receives surety about his next steps, and this "aha" experience is visible on his face. Notably, Luke does not say that Jesus was transfigured; rather, that "his face changed in appearance." Like Moses, whose face was radiant after being with God on Mount Sinai (Exod 34:29), and Hannah, whose face was lifted up after her prayer was heard (1 Sam 1:18), so Jesus' encounter with God is written on his face. He comes to understand that, indeed, he is to go to Jerusalem, and that he will be put to death there, but his death will not be the end of his life and mission. Rather, his exit from earthly life will bring the new liberation for God's people. The Greek word *exodos* (9:31) literally means "exit," connoting "death" (2 Pet 1:15), and also evokes the liberation of the Israelites from slavery.

During this intense prayer of discernment, Jesus is given sure signs that he is guided by God in his choice. A cloud, the sign of God's presence with the Israelites as they went forth from Egypt, overshadows him, as at his baptism. Two heavenly messengers embody the divine presence, giving Jesus strength as he leans on God's word in the law and the prophets. The heavenly voice reassures both him and his disciples of Jesus' chosen status and the rightness of his choice. Thus assured of God's love and direction, Jesus turns his transformed face toward Jerusalem. Placing his own life in danger, Jesus makes a deliberate, prophetic choice to continue to "proclaim liberty to captives" (4:18, NABRE), as he had declared in his hometown synagogue. His death is not an inevitable fate, but a choice for freeing love.

PRAYING WITH SCRIPTURE

1. When have you been invited to risk your own comfort or security to serve the needs of others?

2. Reflect on how difficult choices for love can be freeing.

3. What does your face reveal about your relationship with God?

I AM WHO I AM

Third Sunday of Lent

Readings: Exod 3:1-8a, 13-15; Ps 103:1-2, 3-4, 6-7, 8, 11; 1 Cor 10:1-6, 10-12; Luke 13:1-9

"I AM the One who causes to be what comes into existence" (Exod 3:14)

(Translation from W. F. Albright, *From Stone Age to Christianity* [Garden City, NY: Doubleday, 1957], 261.)

A well-known evangelical preacher recently pointed a finger at the Haitians, declaring that their own sinfulness had brought down upon them the wrath of God in the form of an earthquake. It's such a simple explanation: if something bad happens, then the victims must have done something to deserve it. That's what Jesus figures people are thinking when they report to him about the people whom Pilate murdered and the people who were killed when a tower fell on them.

There may, indeed, be sinful causes behind these events, but not on the part of the victims. Pilate, who carries out violent execution of innocent people, embodies a sin-wracked system. Deaths caused by shoddy workmanship or construction shortcuts, when profit is prized over human safety, are the result of sinful practices, but not those of the ones who fall victim. In the gospel, Jesus does not answer the more complex question of why bad things happen to good people, but he does clearly dissociate untimely death from sin and guilt. What he emphasizes in his response is the need to always be prepared—the end could come quite unexpectedly. Are you ready?

A dear friend was recently diagnosed with a life-threatening brain tumor. In an instant her life took a dramatic turn, as the possibility of a shortened life faced her. Her response brought many up short. "I can honestly say I have no regrets," she said. The gospel today invites all of us more deeply into such a relationship with God, where we too can say we are ready at any moment, with no regrets.

The gospel also underscores God's patience in waiting for us to repent and "bear fruit." In Luke's Gospel, repentance does not come about by human efforts at reforming our lives. Rather, the process of transformation begins with God's gracious initiative. Our Lenten practices help to sharpen our ability to be transformed and to respond in such ways that can set us ablaze with divine love, like the bush that caused Moses to turn aside and look.

The examples of people dying in unexpected tragic ways are not meant to scare us into repentance. They are a sobering reminder, however, that our time to respond to the divine invitation is limited. We would not want to miss the opportunity to enter more deeply into the heart of "the One who causes to be what comes into existence," as renowned biblical scholar William F. Albright translated the mysterious divine name in Exodus 3:14.

There is no adequate explanation for sudden, tragic death. Nor is there any adequate way to speak of the One Who Is and Who Causes All to Be. Yet we long for precise answers to our most difficult questions. Moses insists that he needs to be able to tell the Israelites who it is that sent him. But God rightly resists any limitations of human categorization. In ancient cultures it was thought that knowing another's name gave you power over that one. Not only can we not have power over God, but any words or images we use are completely inadequate to put into speech who and what God is. Any image falls short and captures only a glimpse of our experience of the ever-expanding power of love that emanates from the Cause of All Being. As we journey in Lent with those who are being initiated into the faith, it is a good time to let go of any overconfidence, as Paul admonishes the Corinthians, allowing ourselves to be enveloped in mystery, to be fashioned anew by the One Who Causes All to Be.

PRAYING WITH SCRIPTURE

1. Allow God to reveal to you a new name for Holy Mystery. Try it out in your prayer.

2. If the end of your earthly life were near, would you be ready?

3. How do you experience God's patience with you?

CLAIMING OUR INHERITANCE

Fourth Sunday of Lent

Readings: Josh 5:9a, 10-12; Ps 23:1-3a,
3b-4, 5, 6; 2 Cor 5:17-21; Luke 15:1-3, 11-32

"[E]verything I have is yours" (Luke 15:32)

One often hears of bitter disputes among siblings when it comes time to divide up the inheritance left by their parents. The parable Jesus tells begins on a shocking note—the younger brother demands his share before the father is even dead! The older brother stands there mute as the father, without a word of protest, gives each son his share. The elder brother's objections come later, when his brother returns home and the former fears his own portion will be jeopardized. Both sons display a sense of entitlement. They have calculated what they have coming to them and they are making sure they collect all of it. There is a considerable amount of inheritance involved. This is not a poor family. They have cattle and means to put on a feast. The father has a fine robe, sandals, and a ring to put on his son.

When the father hands over his considerable wealth to his sons, one would think they would be happy. But both end up miserable. The younger one squanders everything, while the older one hoards it all, not spending even a little bit to entertain his friends. Both complain about what they have not been given. The younger son, after using up all he had inherited, lowers his sights and would be satisfied with the slop fed to the swine, "but nobody gave him any." The elder son complains bitterly to his father, "you never gave me even a young goat to feast on with my friends." This accusation is puzzling, when the son has already been given everything the father has. It is equally surprising that the father, instead of angrily dismissing his son's baseless accusations, responds with a renewed invitation to joy, and a reminder: "everything I have is yours"—already! But something has died in both sons. Their greed and jealousy have blinded them to the overflowing abundance that is theirs.

The first son has come back to life. He has hit rock bottom, believes he no longer deserves to be called "son," and acknowledges the wrong he has done his father and the whole community. What has brought him back to life is not his own coming to his senses and his own efforts to return to the source of his heritage. Rather, it is the father's unfailing love, as he seeks him out and flings open his arms, wrapping him in a mantle of forgiveness, that resurrects in him the response of love and joy and gratitude, along with the sure knowledge that all is given freely and totally. This heritage cannot be earned and it is never depleted, even by our most egregious misuses.

As a figure of the divine, the father offers a gift of reconciliation that shatters the too narrow vision of children vying for a bigger piece of the pie, when all along the whole of the inheritance is offered to each and all, with no bounds. This gift begins a process of healing that expands our puny estimation of our inheritance and opens our capacity to be transformed by the Giver, enlarging our capacity to pass on that heritage to others.

Paul talks about this process as a "new creation." The One who created an ever-expanding universe is ever drawing us deeper into the divine embrace, so as to extend that heritage outward in ever-widening circles. The question that is left unanswered at the end of the gospel parable is whether or not the older son can accept the inheritance being offered to him. The father will not give up on his son, who is filled with joyless resentment as he calculates what is owed him. The Source of grace and compassion will wait as long as it takes for transformative love to do its re-creative work.

PRAYING WITH SCRIPTURE

1. Talk with God about what is dead in you that longs to come to life again.

2. What inheritance does God want you to claim right now?

3. Ask Christ to help you let go of any resentment toward others with whom you share this inheritance.

THE FINGER OF GOD

Fifth Sunday of Lent

Readings: Isa 43:16-21;
Ps 126:1-2, 2-3, 4-5, 6; Phil 3:8-14; John 8:1-11

"Jesus bent down and began to write on the ground with his finger" (John 8:6)

It is so easy to point a finger at someone caught red-handed in a sinful act. While someone else is in the spotlight, the chances diminish that my own wrongdoings will be found out and draw others' attention—at least for the moment. Joining the mob of accusers also keeps me from self-examination, and the possibility of repentance. It's much easier to point out other peoples' shortcomings.

In the gospel today the case seems clear-cut. A woman is caught in the very act of adultery. The evidence is indisputable and the law is clear. It is just a matter of carrying it out. Jesus' opponents are not interested in the circumstances that led to the woman's actions—and one must wonder how her partner escaped judgment when both were caught in the act! The scribes and Pharisees are intent on being able to charge Jesus with transgressing the law. They quote the law of Moses to Jesus and press him for his judgment. While they wait for an answer Jesus bends down and begins to write on the ground with his finger.

Much ink has been spilt by commentators who speculate on what Jesus wrote. Saint Jerome proposed that it was the sins of the accusers. Others suggest that Jesus was imitating Roman legal practice, where the judge first writes the sentence and then reads it aloud. Still others propose that Jesus is doodling, buying time while he ponders his response. I suggest that the Evangelist is making a connection with the giving of the law to Moses.

Exodus 31:18 says, "When God finished speaking with Moses on Mount Sinai, he gave him the two tablets of the covenant, tablets of stone, written with the finger of God" (NRSV). It is not the content of Jesus' writing that is important; otherwise the Evangelist would have told us what it said. It

29

is Jesus' action of writing with his finger, replicating God's action in the giving of the law, that helps us understand that Jesus' interpretation of the law is in line with God's intent. The law was never intended as an instrument of condemnation but was to guide believers in a godly way of life.

Like Jesus' opponents in the gospel, Christian teachers and preachers have struggled to understand how Jesus could let a blatant sinner off without punishment. Saint Ambrose worried that the gospel could produce anxiety in the inexperienced and tried to dismiss the idea that Jesus could have made a mistake. John Calvin assured his followers that although Jesus remits our sins, he does not subvert the social order or abolish legal sentences and punishments. While the latter may be true, Jesus does, indeed, abolish the notion that our relationship with God is contained within rules and law. While these are necessary for the peaceable ordering of any organization, whether civil or religious, law does not express adequately how we relate with God. It is God's freely given gift of forgiveness, offered to us in the person of Christ, that binds us to God and invites us to a new way of life. It is a gift that is replicated every time we offer forgiveness and compassion to one another.

A marvelous image is given to us by Michelangelo on the ceiling of the Sistine Chapel in Rome: God, surrounded by cherubs, with his left arm draped around a female figure, strains his right arm forward, with his index finger extended toward Adam. Instead of pointing the finger of guilt at humankind, God is exerting every effort to draw the human creature into the divine loving embrace. Their fingers almost touch. If he wanted to, Adam could complete the connection.

PRAYING WITH SCRIPTURE

1. While you pray, keep in mind the image of the finger of God that points toward compassion rather than condemnation.

2. How might you be holding back from touching the finger of God?

3. What does Jesus say to you when you face him in prayer with your sins?

OBEDIENT UNTO DEATH

Palm Sunday of the Lord's Passion

Readings: Isa 50:4-7; Ps 22:8-9, 17-18,
19-20, 23-24; Phil 1:6-11; Luke 22:14–23:56

*"This is my body, which will be given for you;
do this in memory of me"* (Luke 22:19)

I remember as a child looking at gruesome pictures of the crucified Jesus in our family Bible. I was very disturbed by them, but I found comfort in thinking that since Jesus was God he didn't feel the suffering in the same way we would. I also knew that he was unique and thought that what happened to him would not happen to anybody else. The gospel, however, makes very clear that what Jesus underwent as a rejected prophet can, indeed, be asked of any of his disciples. In addition, it portrays for us how to prepare for and how to endure suffering that comes from following in his footsteps.

Luke, more than the other evangelists, emphasizes Jesus' role as prophet and interprets the death of Jesus as rejection of his prophetic teaching and actions. Like all prophets, Jesus is lauded by those lifted up by his good news, but those whose privileged position is threatened by him seek to silence and kill him. In the passion narrative, we see Jesus facing deadly opposition and struggling one final time to discern what is the way to obediently bring his prophetic mission to completion. He prepares his disciples for his own death, instructing them at the Last Supper, and modeling for them how they are to act, as they continue his prophetic mission.

At Gethsemane, Jesus is kneeling upright, not prostrate on the ground, as Matthew and Mark portray him. He is in *agonia*, or agony, which connotes intense struggle, like an athlete, straining every muscle, sweating so profusely it is as if a vein were opened. He can see what will be the consequences if he stays the course. He still has an option to retreat over the Mount of Olives, and into the Judean desert. As at other turning points in his life, like his baptism and transfiguration, he feels God's reassuring presence with him, strengthening him for what lies ahead.

Once again he chooses to be obedient to the prophetic mission entrusted to him, even if the cost is his life. It is in this sense that Paul speaks of Jesus as "obedient even unto death." It is not obedience to a father who wills his son to die—for what parent would ever wish such a fate on their child? Rather, Jesus' obedience is to divine love for all humanity and to the prophetic mission to release all who are bound by sin and suffering, bringing jubilee freedom to all. It is a costly love that impels him.

At the Last Supper Jesus interprets his impending death, saying to his disciples, "This is my body . . . given for you." In Luke, this gift is not one act that is thought to atone for sins but rather a life-long self-surrender in service to the least. It is manifest in acts of healing and forgiveness right up until Jesus' last moments, when his final words are a prayer for God to forgive his executioners, and of entrusting himself peacefully into God's hands (using Psalm 31), in contrast to the anguished cry of abandonment of the Markan Jesus (using Psalm 22).

As followers of such a prophet, our own obedience is modeled on his. First, prophetic obedience is enacted by turning one's ear to God morning after morning, to hear how to speak a rousing word to the weary, as Isaiah says. It also entails remembering, as Jesus said at the Last Supper—making present again his bold words and freeing actions of healing and forgiveness. As servant leaders, it also means going, like the Galilean women, to the places of death, keeping watch in solidarity with the crucified peoples of our world and continuing to protest the machinery of death, even as we ourselves risk falling victim to it.

PRAYING WITH SCRIPTURE

1. How have you felt God's strengthening presence in times when you have struggled to know God's will?

2. Pray for the gift to give and seek forgiveness wherever it is needed.

3. How do you protest the machinery of death? At what risk to yourself?

BEYOND HOPE

Easter Sunday

Readings: Acts 10:34a, 37-43; Ps 118:1-2, 16-17, 22-23;
Col 3:1-4; Luke 24:13-35 (one of three options)

"[W]e were hoping that he would be the one to redeem Israel" (Luke 24:21)

Some years ago my mom and I took a trip to the Grand Canyon. We drove from Chicago, stopping along the way, whenever something took our fancy. There were chance encounters with people who offered spontaneous kindness, and others whose rudeness challenged us not to respond in kind. When we reached our destination, the experience was indescribable—far beyond what we could imagine, and impossible to capture in words or photos. There were experienced trail guides and interpretive signs, but what we saw was far beyond what the geological explanations could tell. We sat gazing in hushed awe. Words would do a disservice to the immense beauty that engulfed us.

In a similar fashion, no words are capable of expressing what happened to Jesus at Easter, or what happened to the first disciples who experienced him as resurrected. The only adequate response is contemplative awe, yet we need to try to say something of what this experience means for us.

In the gospel story today, two of Jesus' disciples are talking and debating as they walk away from Jerusalem, the place of pain and confusion, trying to make meaning of it all. They are struggling to see how to make sense, but cannot yet do so. As Jesus joins them, he first elicits from them their own interpretation. They retell what they experienced of Jesus as "a prophet mighty in deed and word before God and all the people," and they recount the truth of his brutal murder. They speak of what their hopes were, but these now seem dashed. They tell about what some of the women experienced at the tomb and their interpretation that Jesus was alive. Others went to see for themselves, finding the tomb empty, but they did not see him alive as the women had.

Different disciples are at different stages in their journey with and toward the risen One, each seeing something different and each needing to interpret it in their own words.

It is remarkable that Jesus does not immediately interpret for Cleopas and his companion what their journey with him means. Then, as now, Jesus first asks disciples to try to say what they (or we) have experienced and how we understand what has happened. This first step takes us only part of the way.

To go the next step on the journey it is necessary to turn to the Scriptures—the official guidebook, if you will—which help to unravel the meaning. Immersing ourselves in the whole story, from Moses through all the prophets, we understand a little more of Jesus' prophetic life and mission. We see too how we are asked to conform our own lives to this journey of prophetically embodying good news for the most vulnerable, being prepared to accept its cost. Essential for this journey is the abiding presence of the risen Jesus. As did those first disciples, we too implore him to stay with us. And he does. He continues to open our eyes by unfolding the Scriptures to us and by making himself known in the breaking of the bread.

No words adequately express our experience of what it is like to have him risen among us. Resurrected life far exceeds all our hopes and is far more than a happy ending to a tragic story. It is not only what happened to Jesus, but is already lived by us, whose lives are "hidden with Christ in God," as Paul says. It is not only the end of a life's journey, but is tasted already now, all along the way. It is beyond all that we had hoped, and even now sets our hearts burning within us.

PRAYING WITH SCRIPTURE

1. Ask the risen One to stay with you and to open your eyes.

2. Who are the women today who keep vigil in places of death? What visions do they announce?

3. How is the risen Christ setting your heart burning within you?

HELD FAST IN PEACE

Second Sunday of Easter

Readings: Acts 5:12-16; Ps 118:2-4,
13-15, 22-24; Rev 1:9-11a, 12-13, 17-19; John 20:19-31

"Whomever you hold fast are held fast" (John 20:23; my translation)

In 1989 Sister Thea Bowman was invited to speak to the US bishops about
the needs of the black Catholic community. At the end of her address, she
asked the bishops to sing with her and to link arms, as in the days of civil
rights marches. Weakened from the cancer that took her life the following
year, she nonetheless led the bishops with her powerful voice as they joined
her in singing "We Shall Overcome."

She invited them to stand up and reach out and take each other's hands,
which they did. "No, not like that," she admonished, as they tentatively
took one another's hands. "Cross your arms over your chest and then take
the hands on either side," she instructed. "That's how we did it in the civil
rights marches. You have to move in together, close to one another, and
hold on tight so that no one is lost in the struggle."

The instruction to hold on tight to one another is part of Jesus' recurring
message in the Gospel of John. After feeding the multitude, he says that
God's will is that he "should not lose anything" of what has been given
to him (6:39, NABRE). Speaking as a shepherd, he declares that no one
will snatch his sheep out of his hand (10:28). In his final prayer, he says he
guarded all those that the Father had given him and not one of them was
lost (17:12; see also 18:9). In today's gospel, when the risen Christ appears
to the fearful disciples, he empowers them to continue his mission of drawing all to himself (12:32) and not allowing any to be lost in the struggle.

Jesus equips the disciples with everything they need to continue his
mission. First, he opens the locked doors of their hearts to recognize that
he is standing in their midst. He had assured them that he would not leave
them orphaned (14:18) and that he would abide always with them (15:4-10).

He had also told them he would give them a peace unlike the peace that the world gives (14:27).

As the risen Christ stands in their midst, we see that his peace comes from letting go of fear and the desire for vengeance and from surrounding the violence with forgiveness and reconciliation. This kind of peace does not ignore the brutal suffering inflicted on the victim. Jesus holds out his wounded hands and side as evidence that is never erased. The pain from the violence can be transformed, however, into joy and peace, through the power of the Spirit and through the abiding presence of Christ, who makes forgiveness possible.

The disciples are not to stay huddled together in fear behind locked doors, but are sent by Christ to continue his mission of healing and forgiving. Just as the Creator breathed life into the nostrils of the first human creature, making it into a living being (Gen 2:7), so Jesus breathes life into the disciples, empowering them to forgive everything and everyone they can. The second half of verse 23, usually translated "whose sins you retain are retained," does not have the word *sins* in the Greek text. A better way to understand it is "whomever you hold fast are held fast." The sense is that through processes of forgiveness and reconciliation, disciples of Jesus continue his mission of holding on to all, arms folded across our chests, clenching each hand tightly, so that none, especially the most vulnerable, are lost in the struggle.

Not all follow the same process toward embracing the peace Christ extends. As the scene with Thomas affirms, disciples encounter the risen Christ at different times and in different ways. Some come to believe through seeing and through signs, others without these visible means. Both ways are blessed and lead to life in his name.

PRAYING WITH SCRIPTURE

1. Ask the risen One to breathe new life in whatever area needs his empowering Spirit.

2. Pray for the gift of forgiveness that can unleash peace and joy.

3. How do you experience the abiding presence of the risen Christ?

ARMS OUTSTRETCHED

Third Sunday of Easter

Readings: Acts 5:27-32, 40b-41;
Ps 30:2, 4, 5-6, 11-12, 13; Rev 5:11-14; John 21:1-19

"[W]hen you grow old, you will stretch out your hands, and someone else will dress you and lead you where you do not want to go" (John 21:18)

At a recent liturgy, a couple who had been married for fifty years came forward and renewed their marital promises to one another. Similarly, at the yearly gathering of our congregation, we sisters publicly renew our vows before returning to our mission. The commitment to love is not something professed only once, but again and again. Recalling one's first fervor of infatuation with the beloved fans into flame again the ability to continue loving despite hardships and challenges.

So it is with Peter in today's gospel. When pressed by a servant girl in the courtyard of the high priest, he had failed to acknowledge that he even knew Jesus, much less that he loved and believed in him. Earlier, at the tumultuous moment of Jesus' arrest, he had hotheadedly lashed out with a sword and had cut off the ear of a slave of the high priest. His failures to love are symbolically depicted in his inability to catch any fish.

Yet Peter still does love Jesus, and is still able to bring many others into that circle of love. Allowing himself to be fed by the Source of love, he experiences forgiveness, renewal, and empowerment to extend that love to others. It is an efficacious and uniting love, symbolized by the great haul of fish and the net that is not torn.

Three times Peter professes his love. Three is a complete number, signaling fullness. Some commentators note that there are two different Greek words for love in this exchange between Jesus and Peter. The first two times Jesus uses the verb *agapaō*, signaling the kind of Christian love that is totally self-giving and inclusive. Both times Peter responds with the verb *phileō*, which refers to the love of friends. The third time Jesus switches to *phileō*, to which Peter again responds with *phileō*.

Some commentators think of this shift in vocabulary as Peter's inability to achieve the highest form of love that Jesus asks, and that Jesus comes down to Peter's level the third time. More likely is that the Evangelist is simply varying the vocabulary, as is the case with the verbs for feed (*boskein*, vv. 15, 17) and tend (*poimainein*, v. 16), and the nouns for lambs (*arnion*, v. 15) and sheep (*probaton*, vv. 16, 17). Moreover, in this gospel, there is no greater love than the love of a friend who lays down his or her life for a friend (15:13).

The love between Jesus and his own is both fruitful and costly. It is not a love that encloses the lovers in an exclusive bubble of bliss. It is a love that bears fruit, extending itself outward in mission, feeding the hungers of those who are most vulnerable. It asks disciples to take a stance of arms outstretched—extended in prayer, in embrace of the Beloved and all his friends, in service to those in need, and finally, in cruciformity—as the outstretched arms of Christ draw all to himself.

PRAYING WITH SCRIPTURE

1. Say a prayer of recommitment to the loving relationships in which you are bound.

2. In what ways are your arms outstretched to and with the Beloved?

WASHED IN THE BLOOD OF THE LAMB

Fourth Sunday of Easter

Readings: Acts 13:14, 43-52;
Ps 100:1-2, 3, 5; Rev 7:9, 14b-17; John 10:27-30

*"[T]hey have washed their robes and made them white
in the blood of the Lamb"* (Rev 7:14)

There are all kinds of detergents that claim to be able to remove the most stubborn of stains. When those fail, home remedies abound. Everyone knows that once a stain is set, it is all the more difficult to get out. The sooner the treatment is applied, the better the chances the mark can be lifted. One of the hardest stains to remove is blood.

In today's reading from the book of Revelation, there appears the startling image of blood as a cleaning agent. The seer recounts a vision of the end time, when a huge multitude, "from every nation, race, people, and tongue," stands together before the throne of the victorious Lamb, bedecked in brilliant white robes. The seer is told that these are "the ones who have survived the time of great distress" and that their robes have been washed "in the blood of the Lamb." The paradox of whiteness resulting from being washed in blood invites us to reflect more deeply on these powerful symbols.

At first we may think of the blood as Christ's atoning, sacrificial blood, which removes the stain of our sin. But in Johannine literature, there are very few traces of atonement theology. The Lamb in the Gospel of John is the Passover lamb, whose bones are not broken (Exod 12:46; John 19:36), and whose blood, as in the exodus, protects his people from the destroyer, and whose flesh fortifies his own for their journey to freedom. This is the one whose blood came forth from his pierced side, along with waters of rebirth (19:34), cleansing, renewing, and opening the way to new life for all. Paradoxically, the Lamb is also the shepherd, whose sheep respond to the sound of his voice, and from whose hands no one can snatch his sheep.

In the book of Revelation, the Lamb is now enthroned in glory, clothing everyone in the resplendent robe of his life and love.

The robes are brilliant white, the color of purity, victory, and innocence. As Sir Isaac Newton showed, the color white combines all the visible colors of light in equal proportions. So too, in the vision of the end times in Revelation, people of every color and race are gathered together into one, not to have their own distinctiveness erased, but for all to be formed into one body, with equal dignity and purity. The blood that washes over each is the life force unleashed by the crucified Jesus and infused into his followers by the Spirit. It does not whitewash the shedding of blood from racism and other forms of sin, but empowers all who are bloodied in the earthly struggles to emerge cleansed in his loving life force.

The seer envisions this life force enduring for all eternity. Those who "remain faithful to the grace of God" (Acts 13:43) are sheltered by the Lamb sitting on the throne. They no longer suffer hunger or thirst, either for physical food, or for justice and peace. The scorching heat of the struggle is past, and overflowing tears are replaced with life-giving springs of water. Even the most stubborn of stains can be overcome when placed in the hands of the victorious Lamb who shepherds us.

PRAYING WITH SCRIPTURE

1. How do you experience the life force of the Lamb of God in you?

2. Pray for the grace to accept all people as equals, since all are clothed in the inclusive love of the Lamb.

LOVE COMMANDED

Fifth Sunday of Easter

Readings: Acts 14:21-27; Ps 145:8-9, 10-11, 12-13; Rev 21:1-5a; John 13:31-33a, 34-35

"I give you a new commandment: love one another" (John 13:34)

Two neighbors had a nasty falling-out a number of years ago. One has reached out to the other over and over: greeting her whenever they pass one another on the street, calling out to her former friend when she would see her in her yard, attempting time after time to mend the breach. Each effort is rebuffed or ignored, and yet the persistent neighbor tries again and again. In many ways these efforts exemplify the kind of love about which Jesus speaks in today's gospel.

Jesus' command to love one another is part of his explanation to the disciples of his washing their feet. He has modeled for them actions that bespeak love—a love that will even go so far as to surrender life itself for the other. It is a love that is extended even to those who will not reciprocate it. Jesus washed the feet of all the disciples—even Judas who was about to hand him over to his opponents, and Peter, who was about to deny he ever knew Jesus.

Throughout the gospel we see that Jesus never gives up on those who oppose him or who do not understand him. He continues to offer them opportunities right to the end. His love could even reach the Roman procurator, Pilate, with whom he engages in lengthy conversation, as he had done with Nicodemus, a Samaritan woman, a man born blind, Martha, and Mary. In those instances, there was an openness that eventually resulted in faith. Even though Pilate would ultimately reject Jesus' love, Jesus nonetheless offers it.

Jesus not only gives the disciples the gift of his love but he also commands them to do as he has done. He has shown what love is by acting it out—pouring out himself in service, even to calamity's depths. When we see Jesus' love in action, it becomes evident how love can be commanded.

In biblical parlance, love does not consist in warm, fuzzy feelings toward another but in visible acts toward others that bespeak common divine parentage and common commitment to one another. To love as Jesus loves, it is not necessary to like or even feel kindly toward the other person. But it is necessary to act toward the other in the way Jesus treated his disciples as he washed their feet. Sometimes loving feelings result from loving action extended and received.

The new creation of which the author of Revelation speaks is not something magical that appears out of the sky. Rather, it begins here and now with each act that aims at fulfilling Jesus' command to love. The refusal to give up on anyone and the refusal to let another's rejection extinguish the offer of love are acts that begin the construction of the new dwelling of God, wherein all tears are wiped away and all pain is salved. The old order of tit-for-tat dissolves, as all that is broken is made new.

This "new Jerusalem" is a place where all can find a home. At the Last Supper, Jesus does not envision a closed circle of mutually exchanged love but one that keeps widening outward. Just as Paul and Barnabas energetically traversed Asia Minor, offering the good news even to Gentiles, so the commandment to love demands that we continue to open our circles, especially to those to whom we are least attracted.

PRAYING WITH SCRIPTURE

1. Talk to Jesus about a strained relationship in your life, and let him show you how to act in love.

2. How have you experienced "the new Jerusalem" already being built?

3. How have Jesus' acts of love toward you empowered you to love others?

THE GIFT OF PEACE

————————————— **Sixth Sunday of Easter**

Readings: Acts 15:1-2, 22-29;
Ps 67:2-3, 5, 6, 8; Rev 21:10-14, 22-23; John 14:23-29

*"[M]y peace I give to you.
Not as the world gives do I give it to you"* (John 14:27)

When people disagree with one another about deeply held convictions, especially those based on religious beliefs, coming to peaceable agreement is no easy task. The vitriolic exchanges and even threats of physical violence that have been voiced in the process of reforming health care in the United States, for example, are quite different from the way the first Christians resolved their differences regarding observance of the Mosaic law in changing circumstances.

Today's first reading abbreviates Luke's description of the process, as it presents the problem, and then jumps to the agreed-upon solution. It is helpful to look at the omitted verses from Acts 15 to see the steps by which communities of faith can accept and live out the gift of peace that Jesus promises his disciples in the gospel.

As the Jesus movement spread outward to include more and more Gentiles, heated debates ensued over whether these newcomers should keep the whole of the Mosaic law. Some said yes, some said no, and others argued for a compromise position: keep some observances, but not others. The next question was inevitable: If Gentile Christians did not need to be circumcised or to observe all the dietary regulations, then should Jewish Christians continue to be bound by them? How would a mixed community be able to eat together if some were keeping kosher and others not?

As Acts 15 recounts, albeit in an idealized way, there came a point when a group from Judea, not authorized by the Jerusalem leaders, came to Antioch, where Paul and Barnabas were recounting all that God was doing through them in their missionary travels among the Gentiles. The Judeans, who were arguing for full observance of the law by Gentiles, created no little dissension and debate, as Paul and Barnabas took them on, holding that Gentiles should not be bound by the law.

In the verses omitted from today's first reading, Luke describes how all the leaders gathered in Jerusalem to resolve the dispute. First there was intense listening to all sides. Paul and Barnabas reported what God had done through them in Gentile lands. Then some of the Pharisees who had become believers spoke of their conviction that the whole law must be observed by all. After much debate, Peter finally stood and put forth a decisive argument: it was apparent that God had given the Holy Spirit to the Gentiles as well as to Jewish Christians, making no distinction between the two. He then argued for a relaxation of observance of the law. Then the leaders listened again to Paul and Barnabas as they described "the signs and wonders God had worked among the Gentiles through them" (15:12, NABRE). Next, James, the leader of the Jerusalem community, quoted a text from Amos 9:11-12, concerning God's ingathering of Gentiles. He then proposed a compromise, as we hear in the remainder of today's first reading.

Through deep and respectful listening to all sides, careful attention to what the Spirit is doing in present experience, study of the Scriptures, reflection on tradition, respectful debate and discussion, silence and prayer, the first Christians arrive at a solution that allowed for communal living in peace among people of differing convictions. This process did not resolve the problem once and for all, but gives us an example of how we might receive and live from the gift of peace given to us by the risen Christ.

PRAYING WITH SCRIPTURE

1. Listen to the promptings of the Spirit as you bring to prayer a situation of conflict in need of peaceful resolution.

2. How is the gift of peace both freely given and empowering and yet costly in its demands?

3. Ask the Spirit for the gift of a nondefensive, listening heart.

CLOTHED WITH POWER

The Ascension of the Lord

Readings: Acts 1:1-11; Ps 47:2-3,
6-7, 8-9; Heb 9:24-28; 10:19-23; Luke 24:46-53

"[S]tay in the city until you are clothed with power from on high" (Luke 24:49)

In her book *Wouldn't Take Nothing for My Journey Now* (Random House, 1993), poet laureate Maya Angelou tells of her memory of her grandmother who raised her in the little town of Stamps, Arkansas. She describes her as "a tall cinnamon-colored woman with a deep, soft voice," whose difficult life caused her to rely utterly on the power of God. Angelou envisioned Mamma "standing thousands of feet up in the air on nothing visible," when she would draw herself up to her full six feet, clasp her hands behind her back, look up into a distant sky, and declare, "I will step out on the word of God." Maya continues, "She would look up as if she could will herself into the heavens, and tell her family in particular and the world in general, 'I will step out on the word of God.'" "Immediately," Angelou recalls, "I could see her flung into space, moons at her feet and stars at her head, comets swirling around her. Naturally it wasn't difficult for me to have faith. I grew up knowing that the word of God has power" (pp. 73–74).

In today's readings, we have similar images of Jesus "taken up" into the sky, having spent an earthly lifetime stepping out on the word of God. The disciples want to know if now is the time that he is going to restore the kingdom to Israel (Acts 1:6). They have hopes and expectations for the future fixed in past experiences of God's saving hand in their history. Jesus does not directly answer their question, but points them to the power of the Holy Spirit, with which they will be clothed. This power will guide them so that they will be able to step out on the word that has been entrusted to them, courageously witnessing to the gospel from Jerusalem to the ends of the earth. As Jesus himself learned in his earthly sojourn, the *what* and the *when* of the mission cannot fully be known, but only the *Who* that wraps them in the mantle of divine love.

What Jesus instructs the disciples to proclaim is that God holds out to all people the priceless raiment of divine forgiveness and asks in return only that they let themselves be clothed with power from on high to turn away from anything that stands between them and the divine clothier. Disciples are not to stand looking up into the sky, gazing after the One who has now been taken up. Their work is to teach others that same trust in the power of the word to uphold them and clothe them with power.

Although Luke depicts the ascension as a separate event that occurs forty days after the resurrection, in the first centuries the church did not treat it either in its writings or in its liturgies as a separate happening from the resurrection. Rather, the passion, death, resurrection, ascension, glorification, and giving of the Spirit are all various facets of one moment. Luke, in fact, as we see in today's readings, tells the story of the ascension twice: once at the end of the gospel, as occurring on the day of resurrection, and again at the beginning of the Acts of the Apostles, as happening forty days later. It is one grand act of God, one word on which we step out, one power that clothes us, until the day we too are taken into the divine realm forever.

PRAYING WITH SCRIPTURE

1. How do you experience the divine power that clothes you?

2. What does it mean to "step out on the word of God"?

3. How do you spread the message of repentance and forgiveness?

COMING HOME

Seventh Sunday of Easter

Readings: Acts 7:55-60; Ps 97:1-2, 6-7, 9;
Rev 22:12-14, 16-17, 20; John 17:20-26

"I am coming soon" (Rev 22:20)

A few years ago the movie *Cold Mountain* came out, telling the story of a Civil War soldier who had fallen in love just before he marched off to war. The movie portrays his grueling trek home to be reunited with his beloved, only to be tragically killed just after he reaches her.

In today's gospel, we have the third and last part of Jesus' prayer just before he completes the final part of his journey back to the One who sent him. In the Fourth Gospel Jesus frequently speaks of his earthly sojourn in terms of descending and ascending, of having been sent from and returning to the Father. Paradoxically, he also speaks of never having been parted from the Father. From the opening lines of the gospel, we are told that the Logos is one with God (1:1) and is ever in the bosom of the Father (1:18).

In today's gospel passage Jesus speaks of his profound oneness with the Father that he desires to share completely with those who believe in him. Unlike the parted lovers in *Cold Mountain*, who treasured tattered photos of each other close to their hearts until they would be physically united again, with Jesus and the One who sent him there was never any physical parting.

The unity of Jesus with the Father is not that of an exclusive twosome. Jesus' fervent prayer is that all may be drawn into this uniting love of the divine persons. He prays not only for those who have come to believe in him but also for all who will believe through their word, as he earnestly desires "that they may all be one, as you, Father, are in me and I in you, that they also may be in us" (17:21).

As we are becoming more aware in our day of the oneness of the whole cosmos, we may hear Jesus' prayer not only for oneness of the human community but also for every part of the created universe. We know that

47

every part of the cosmos is interrelated and connected in one great web of life and that we are physically connected by atoms that have recycled into us from other living beings.

Since this is our reality, perhaps Jesus' prayer is not so much a prayer that unity may come to be, but rather that we who are already completely and irrevocably united may come to this realization and act accordingly. This realization would have a profound effect not only on how human beings treat one another but also on the ways in which human beings care for Earth and all creatures.

This oneness that already binds us together is a gift from God, and like all gifts, it can be accepted or rejected. One way in which we can receive the gift is to enter into contemplative prayer, seeking and longing for oneness with our Beloved.

In the first reading we see Stephen looking intently up to heaven, and he sees the glory of God. While God is not to be found physically up in the heavens, this expression captures his deliberate intent to seek God and experience the nearness of God's loving and uniting presence. Stephen's murderers, by contrast, cover their ears so that they will not hear the whispers of love emanating from the Divine and radiating through Stephen. As Stephen completes his earthly journey, he refuses to renounce his union with his executioners, as he prays, as did Jesus, for forgiveness for them.

The author of Revelation, in the second reading, provides us a mantra by which we may pray for oneness. The word *come* is like a drumbeat, inviting us to pray again and again to let our Beloved come and transform us with unifying love. Unlike the tragic ending of *Cold Mountain*, there is nothing to inhibit this uniting love coming to full flourishing in us if we continually pray for it.

PRAYING WITH SCRIPTURE

1. Listen to the voice of the Spirit in the beauty of creation, and let yourself feel oneness with Earth and all creatures.

2. Use the word *come* as a mantra, inviting the unifying divine love to come to perfection in you.

3. If there is some relationship that is ruptured, pray for forgiveness so that uniting love may do its healing work.

BREATH OF GOD

Readings: Acts 2:1-11; Ps 104:1, 24, 29-30, 31, 34;
1 Cor 12:3b-7, 12-13; John 20:19-23 or John 14:15-16, 23b-26

"[H]e breathed on them and said to them,
'Receive the Holy Spirit'" (John 20:22)

Following the recent coal mine disaster in West Virginia, many news stories focused on the dangers of mining and the risks miners face, like being trapped below ground without air or exposing themselves to the possibility of an agonizing death from black lung disease. Those who suffer from breathing difficulties recount how terrifying it is not to be able to catch their breath. And as our consciousness rises about air pollution, we become ever more concerned about the quality of our air, knowing that we cannot live without being able to breathe clean air.

Breath is the very symbol of life and has been since ancient times. Indeed, the first creation account in Genesis depicts the life force of the Creator as *ruah*, meaning "breath" or "wind," which swept over the face of the primordial waters. And in the second account of creation, the first human creature becomes a living being only when the Creator breathes the breath of life into its nostrils (Gen 2:7). At Pentecost, it is this same divine life force that re-creates a frightened group of disciples into bold proclaimers of the gospel.

The symbols of divine presence described in Acts 2 are familiar from the Old Testament: thundering noise, as God's manifestation at Sinai; a whirlwind, like that from which God spoke to Job (Job 38:1); and flames of fire, such as Moses saw at Mount Horeb (Exod 3:2). As in previous times of critical need, God's presence is visible and audible, profoundly transforming those who experience it. The disciples, like anyone who has experienced the death of a loved one, would have felt that something of their own spirit and zest for life had also been snuffed out with Jesus' death. Huddled together, trying to comfort one another, they were unable to muster any

49

energy for carrying on his mission. Grief and fear had deflated any impetus to continue the movement into which he had drawn them.

In both gospel choices for today, we have a glimpse of some concrete ways in which the Spirit brings them and us back to life so as to go forth again in mission. In John 14, Jesus is telling his disciples before his passion that he will not leave them alone. He promises to send the Paraclete to be always with them. Only the Fourth Evangelist uses this term for the Spirit. It comes from the legal world, and connotes one who stands alongside another, as advocate, or as comforter. Not only does the Paraclete teach the disciples and remind them of everything Jesus told them, but this consoling one is as near as one's own breath. When Jesus speaks to those whom he loves of their oneness with him and with the One who sent him, he speaks of mutual indwelling.

In John 20, the risen Christ breathes on the disciples and infuses them with the Spirit. He unleashes in them the power of the Spirit, who alone can bring peace and joy in the wake of terrifying woundedness. He directs them to open themselves to the gift of the Spirit that allows them to receive and give forgiveness. For it is only through the power of forgiveness that the air can be cleared and all can breathe in the peace for which we so long and which the risen One desires to give.

Perhaps it is breath that best signals this intimacy. God, in the person of Jesus and the power of the Spirit, is as close to each and every believer as is our very breath, taken deeply into our lungs thousands of times every day, a constant vivifying force. Just as breath must be exhaled, and cannot be kept within, so too does the Spirit's power direct us outward to mission, exuding the love, peace, and forgiveness we have inhaled from the Living One.

PRAYING WITH SCRIPTURE

1. Focus on your breathing, and as you inhale and exhale, remember the gifts of the Spirit that you receive and with which you minister.

2. What actions can be taken to ensure the availability of clean air for all?

3. How does the action of the Spirit make possible forgiveness and understanding among diverse peoples?

WHAT IS MINE IS YOURS

**The Solemnity
of the Most Holy Trinity**

Readings: Prov 8:22-31;
Ps 8:4-5, 6-7, 8-9; Rom 5:1-5; John 16:12-15

"Everything that the Father has is mine" (John 16:15)

Mi casa es su casa, "My home is your home," is the greeting extended to visitors in many Hispanic households. The hospitality offered is boundless, as hosts outdo themselves in generosity, eager to share with guests everything they have. Most humbling is the way in which communities that have little more than tortillas, rice, and beans as daily fare will find a way to add a bit of meat or other delicacies when guests are present, expending their last resources to ensure the comfort of the visitor.

In some ways this example of persons who pour out themselves in generosity to others gives us a glimpse of the relationship among the persons of the Trinity and of their outpouring of love for us. In today's gospel reading Jesus has been speaking with his disciples about the Paraclete that will come when he departs. As he describes all that the Paraclete, the Spirit, will be and do, we recognize these as the very things that comprised Jesus' person and mission. Jesus explains that the Spirit "will take from what is mine and declare it to you." But what is Jesus' is also what is the Father's, as Jesus asserts, "Everything that the Father has is mine." There is no "yours and mine" in the Godhead—only "ours," as the three interweave in a communion of love in which there is no possessiveness.

Along with the lack of possessiveness that characterizes the Trinity, there are likewise no claims of priority. As the first reading asserts, Wisdom was present at the creation of the cosmos, at the side of the Creator, as a skilled artisan. The opening verse is sometimes translated, "The LORD possessed me, the beginning of his ways" (NAB Lectionary), reflecting the usual meaning of the Hebrew verb *qana*, "to acquire." But here the context

51

implies acquisition by birth so that the verse is better rendered, "The LORD created me at the beginning of his work" (NRSV) or "The LORD begot me, the first-born of his ways" (NAB).

The last part of the phrase is also ambiguous. The Hebrew *reshit* can signify temporal priority, "firstborn," or it can connote excellence. The author of Colossians applies this expression, "the firstborn of all creation," to Christ (Col 1:15, NABRE). There are also strong parallels between what is said of Wisdom in Proverbs 8 and what is said of the Logos in the prologue of the Gospel of John, so that Christ is understood as Wisdom Incarnate, preexistent one, participating in the work of the Creator. The Spirit too, which hovered over the watery chaos at the beginning of creation (Gen 1:2), continues to be the re-creative and revivifying force that engenders life in the post-resurrection experience of the disciples. All three persons of the Trinity existed from the beginning and interrelate as equal in being and function, creating, saving, and enlivening all that exists. They invite us to replicate their nonpossessiveness in our relationships, recognizing that nothing I have is mine alone but is "ours" for the common good.

The final verses of the reading from Proverbs capture the utter delight that characterizes the relationship among the members of the Trinity. Just as Wisdom was the Creator's delight, so Wisdom finds delight in the human race and in playing on the surface of Earth. The Holy Three-in-One invites us to share in this playful delight, enjoying the freedom that comes from saying, "Everything I have is yours."

PRAYING WITH SCRIPTURE

1. How do your acts of hospitality replicate the way the members of the Trinity interrelate?

2. Ask the Holy One to help you let go of possessiveness.

3. Pray with Proverbs 8:30. Feel the delight of the Creator and Holy Wisdom in one another, in Earth, and in the human race.

MY BODY FOR YOU

The Solemnity of the
Most Holy Body and Blood of Christ

Readings: Gen 14:18-20;
Ps 110:1, 2, 3, 4; 1 Cor 11:23-26; Luke 9:11b-17

"This is my body that is for you" (1 Cor 11:24)

This time of year is the "wedding season," as young lovers often choose late spring or early summer to celebrate sacramentally their commitment to each other. In an act of profound self-gift they entrust themselves, body, mind, and heart, to one another in loving union.

There is another way in which bodies are given for others: each mother carries her child within her womb for nine months, sharing her own body and blood for the nourishment of the new life within.

Within the body of believers, church members also give of themselves, body, mind, and spirit, for one another and for the life of the world. In each of the ways in which the whole self is given in love, Jesus' act of self-gift lives on.

In the world of Jesus, the expression "body and blood" was a way of speaking of the whole person. "Body," *sōma*, connotes the whole physical person, while "blood," *haima*, is the life force (Deut 12:23). Today we speak of "body, mind, and spirit" when referring to the whole self. This feast day celebrates the gift of Christ, whose entire self was entrusted to us, both in his ministry of preaching and healing and in his ultimate act of self-surrender in death. In the ancient formula handed on to Paul and then to us, which we repeat at Eucharist, we are invited to receive the body and blood of Christ that is for us and to "do this in remembrance" of him. "Do this" means not only to recall his words and actions at Eucharist but also to emulate his whole manner of life. Moreover, "remembrance" is not simply to call to mind but to make present again Christ's entrusting of himself to us in love.

In the gospel, we see how easy it is to miss the moment when such self-gift is asked of us. The Twelve and the crowd have been with Jesus all day as he has poured out himself in teaching about God's realm and has restored the bodies of those who needed healing. With the day drawing to a close, the peoples' physical needs now come to the fore. The Twelve suggest to Jesus that he send the crowd into the surrounding villages and farms to find lodging and provisions. Such a move would, indeed, give the hosts in the villages the opportunity to give of themselves in eucharistic hospitality.

Instead, Jesus directs the Twelve to their own resources. They are sure there is not enough and they quickly jump to the option of going out and buying provisions. Jesus, however, takes the five loaves and two fish, looks up to heaven, blesses, breaks, and gives them to the disciples to set before the crowd. There is plenty for all and then some. To ask how it happened—Did Jesus actually multiply the loaves and fish, or was it a miracle in which everyone was prompted to share with others what they had brought?—is likely not the question the gospel writer wants us to ask. A better question is: How do we replicate the giving of our whole selves, body, mind, and spirit, to the One who is the Source of all nourishment so that we may be broken open in love for the life of the world?

Such self-giving is not possible on our own. It is in the gathered assembly of believers, where we remember Christ's act in sacramental ritual, that we gain strength and give courage to one another to entrust ourselves to this kind of love. Just as the disciples will have another opportunity at the Last Supper, so we come to the eucharistic table often, so that the ability to replicate Christ's action in our world becomes all the more natural as we remember again and again.

PRAYING WITH SCRIPTURE

1. How have you experienced the gift of Christ's love at Eucharist?

2. Reflect on, and give thanks for, those who have given of themselves for you.

3. Ask the risen Christ to show you how to "do this" in his memory today.

BODILY SPIRITUALITY

The Solemnity of the
Assumption of the Blessed Virgin Mary

Readings: Rev 11:19a; 12:1-6a, 10ab;
Ps 45:10, 11, 12, 16; 1 Cor 15:20-27; Luke 1:39-56

"Christ has been raised from the dead,
the firstfruits of those who have fallen asleep" (1 Cor 15:20)

What happens to us after we die? People in every age wonder whether this present life is all there is. Some bury food and favorite items with their deceased, believing that they will need such things in the afterlife. Some hold that people are reincarnated in another life on Earth. Christians place their hope in resurrected life, with Christ having already preceded us, then raising all who belong to him, as Paul assures the Corinthians in the second reading.

In subsequent verses of this same chapter, Paul speculates on what kind of body we will have at the resurrection. For Paul and other Jews of his day, there could be no existence without a body. Paul speaks of us having transformed, glorious, spiritual, and imperishable bodies, bearing the image of the One who has preceded us in resurrected life.

Today's feast underscores the importance of bodiliness, declaring that Mary, "having completed the course of her earthly life, was assumed body and soul into heavenly glory" (Pius XII, "Munificentissimus Deus," No. 44). For centuries Christians had considered that like other holy figures who had been taken up to heaven—Enoch, Moses, and Elijah (Gen 5:24; Jude 9; 2 Kgs 2:1-12)—Mary would have warranted special attention from God at her death. Many different legends grew up, but it was not until 1950 that Pope Pius XII declared infallibly that the assumption of Mary was a dogma of the Catholic faith.

In today's gospel there is an emphasis on the holiness of the body as a vehicle for the saving life God brings to birth. Both Elizabeth and Mary exemplify an incarnational spirituality, whereby God's action in this world is known through bodiliness. With the infant in her womb leaping for joy, Elizabeth is filled with the Spirit and she pronounces a blessing on Mary and on the child she carries in her body. Mary, in turn, proclaims God's greatness with her whole being (the Greek word *psychē* in verse 46, usually translated "soul," is not a separate part of the human, as opposed to the body, but rather refers to the whole self in all its vitality). Mary prophesies a new world in which there are no longer hungry or exploited bodies.

In a world in which the emperor claimed the titles "Lord," "Savior," and "Mighty One," Mary insists that it is God who saves lowly persons by a liberating power that undoes exploitive imperial systems. In a world in which people were enslaved for revolting against Rome or for debts from excessive taxes, Mary subverts systems of slavery by presenting herself as an empowered person who chooses to serve. She is not a person upon whom servitude is imposed. In a world where the majority struggled to have enough to eat, Mary sings of a time when all who are poor are filled to the full with the good things of God.

In a time when sexual humiliation and exploitation of women was rampant, Mary dreams of God lifting up to dignity all the "lowly." (The Greek verb *tapeinoō*, translated as "lowly" in vv. 48 and 52, is used often in the Septuagint to refer to the sexual humiliation of a woman, as in the case of the rape of Dinah, [Gen 34:2]; the abuse of the concubine of the Levite [Judg 19:24; 20:5]; Amnon's rape of Tamar [2 Kgs 13:12-32]; and the ravishing of the wives in Zion and the maidens in the cities of Judah by the enemy [Lam 5:11].) In the world to come, incipient already in the present time and exemplified by Mary, transformation includes the whole embodied person.

PRAYING WITH SCRIPTURE

1. Give thanks for the body you have been given and pray for the gift of reverence for all bodies.

2. In what ways does Mary's *Magnificat* invite you to embody now what Christians long for in the fullness of God's reign?

3. How do care of the body and care of the soul go hand in hand?

A GREAT CLOUD OF WITNESSES

The Solemnity of All Saints

Readings: Rev 7:2-4, 9-14;
Ps 24:1-2, 3-4, 5-6; 1 John 3:1-3; Matt 5:1-12a

"I had a vision of a great multitude, which no one could count" (Rev 7:9)

In her short story "Revelation," Flannery O'Connor tells of Mrs. Turpin, an upright, if not self-righteous, woman, who gives thanks to God for not having made her like so many other people upon whom she looks down. There is a disturbing incident in a doctor's office that rattles her. A young woman calls her "an old warthog from hell" and tries to choke her. That evening as Mrs. Turpin watches the sunset at the edge of her hog pen, she has a vision of a "vast swinging bridge extending upward from the earth through a field of living fire. Upon it a vast horde of souls were rumbling toward heaven" (*The Complete Stories of Flannery O'Connor* [New York: Farrar, Strauss and Giroux, 1982], 508). Mrs. Turpin sees a whole parade of the most unexpected and motley people, all clapping and leaping and shouting hallelujah. Bringing up the rear were herself and her husband and other people like them.

Today's feast, in like manner, celebrates the whole company of saints, including all those not recognized by name in the church calendar, all those who are part of the great multitude that now leaps for joy eternally in God's presence, shouting hallelujah!

The author of the book of Revelation describes a vision not too different from Mrs. Turpin's: people of every nation, race, people, and tongue are there, purified and robed in white, waving palm branches in gestures of thanks and victory, crying out exuberantly, acclaiming the salvation that comes from God. There are so many that they cannot be counted. All have the protective divine seal emblazoned on their foreheads, marked as God's own beloved possession. They include 144,000 from every tribe of the children of Israel. This is not a limited number but rather a symbolic number for a vast group that cannot be counted. It is a multiple of 12—the full number of the tribes of Israel and the representative number of Jesus' disciples in the renewed Israel, times 1,000, an unimaginably large number in antiquity.

At the end of the reading from Revelation the question is posed: "Who are these wearing white robes, and where did they come from?" The second reading and the gospel answer in part: These are all the beloved children of God, whose family likeness to the Holy One is now revealed. They are the ones who have been poor in spirit, have mourned without comfort, have longed for their inheritance with meekness, have hungered and thirsted unsated for justice, have been merciful and clean of heart, have tried to build peace, and have suffered for all these choices. Their striving to live this way in imitation of Jesus has not always been perfect. They have stumbled and erred but have asked forgiveness and have tried again. They are the ones whom others may never have thought of as saints but who have placed their trust and hope in God, knowing that only by God's grace can they be washed clean and clothed in radiance. Many people, not only people like Mrs. Turpin, may be surprised to find themselves among this heavenly multitude.

Today's feast assures us of a place within this great heavenly chorus when we accept the grace of being sealed as God's own and then choose to live in accord with that grace. It also reminds us that none of us is an only child. We belong to an immense family, a great cloud of witnesses, who constantly surround us and are in communion with us, praying for us and with us, urging us onward toward our final reunion with God and them.

PRAYING WITH SCRIPTURE

1. As you pray today, feel the great cloud of witnesses that surrounds you and upholds you.

2. Give thanks for having been "sealed by the living God."

3. Ask for the grace to live the Beatitudes more completely.

OPEN YOUR GIFT

Second Sunday in Ordinary Time

Readings: Isa 62:1-5;
Ps 96:1-2, 2-3, 7-8, 9-10; 1 Cor 12:4-11; John 2:1-11

"To each is given the manifestation of the Spirit for the common good."
(1 Cor 12:7, NRSV)

In the United States, a soon-to-be married couple usually registers at a major department store for the gifts they would most like to receive for their wedding. They choose the pattern of china they like, the glassware, and silverware. They list small appliances and other useful items for the home they desire. Friends and relatives choose gifts for the couple from among these items, and the store keeps track of whether or not someone else has already purchased them. It is a very efficient system, not at all like the way the Spirit gives gifts.

There is no predictability about how the Spirit distributes the various charisms. One might ask God for a particular gift, and it may or may not be granted. A totally unexpected gift might land in one's lap, bringing surprise and delight—something you might never have thought to ask for, something that ends up a perfect fit! Sometimes there are unsolicited gifts that can seem like white elephants, to be tucked away until a time when they can be "re-gifted."

In the second reading today, Paul lists a whole array of gifts that the Spirit gives, each one carefully chosen for the individual for whom it is intended: wisdom, knowledge, faith, healing, mighty deeds, prophecy, discernment, tongues, interpretation. We might picture the Spirit delighting in choosing a gift for each one—a gift that weds the recipient to the Holy One and impregnates each with God's fruitful power. None of the Spirit's gifts are meant to be kept under wraps. They are always meant to bear fruit, not only in the recipient's life, but also in service toward others.

The wedding scene in today's gospel depicts Jesus as hesitant to open his Spirit-given gifts in public. He thinks the time has not yet come. But, as his mother rightly discerns, the need is urgent. Like all prophets, Jesus is reluctant and objects, just as Jeremiah protested that he was too young, and Moses avowed that he could not speak well. Jesus' mother, however, seems to take on the role of the wedding planner. She works behind the scenes, using her gifts of insight and knowledge, setting the stage for the sign that Jesus will perform. She knows that the time has come for her Son to offer his gifts publicly to bring the marriage between humanity and divinity to consummation.

Just as a wedding is only the beginning of a lifelong love affair, so the sign Jesus performs at Cana is the beginning of his many signs that revealed his glory. It is also the beginning of the disciples' belief in Jesus, who himself is the bridegroom, as John the Baptist acknowledges (John 3:29). The gift of Jesus himself is one that far surpasses any other that we could have on our "wish list"!

PRAYING WITH SCRIPTURE

1. What gifts of the Spirit are most fruitful in you?

2. Who is the Spirit prompting you to call forward to use their gifts?

"GOD INSIDE OUT"

Third Sunday in Ordinary Time

Readings: Neh 8:2-4a, 5-6, 8-10;
Ps 19:8, 9, 10, 15; 1 Cor 12:12-30; Luke 1:1-4; 4:14-21

"The Spirit of the Lord is upon me . . .
to bring glad tidings to the poor" (Luke 4:18)

Many organizations have a mission statement that succinctly defines their purpose. The idea is to be able to state clearly to those on the outside what is the aim of the organization. A mission statement helps as well to keep those within the group focused on their purpose. Luke begins his gospel with his own brief mission statement, telling Theophilus, probably his patron, that he intends to set forth for him an accurate account to give him assurance about the teaching he has received. Today's gospel then jumps ahead to Jesus' declaration of his mission in his hometown synagogue.

Jesus begins by saying that the power of the Holy Spirit is upon him. The Spirit is actually God's mission statement to the world, since prior to Jesus' coming, God's love in mission is first revealed by the Spirit's activity in creation. We can only know the "inside" mystery of God through the "outside" manifestation of the action and presence of the holy in the world and in human experience.

My colleague Stephen Bevans has elaborated a missionary theology of the Spirit, naming it "God Inside Out." Today's gospel says that this Spirit now rests upon Jesus, who makes humanly visible and tangible the inner heart of God, who desires healing, wholeness, and jubilee justice. Luke says that "the eyes of all in the synagogue looked intently" at Jesus when he read from the prophet Isaiah. Could they see "God inside out" as he interpreted the Scripture passage as fulfilled in their hearing?

Similarly, in the first reading, Nehemiah stresses that all the people listened attentively as Ezra read forth the law and interpreted it for them. For our ancestors in the faith, it was through the law that the Spirit made known the inner heart of God. Nehemiah says that "all the people were weeping as they heard the words of the law." He urges them not to be sad or weep but does not explain what caused their weeping.

Were they tears of joy to have returned home from exile in Babylon to their own homeland, with their own temple being rebuilt and their own customs restored? Were they tears of grief over all that had been lost in the intervening years: those who had died or who had not returned with them, the land despoiled, the temple in shambles? Maybe they were tears of repentance. Or were they tears of gratitude for the gift of the law from a God whose words of undeserved love and mercy rained down upon them from the mouth of Ezra? Perhaps the tears were for all of the above. When God reveals outwardly the bounteous heart of divine love, our first response is often to be overwhelmed to the point of tears.

It is easy to imagine that as Jesus announced his embodiment of this divine mission there may have been a similar reaction, as those who felt exiled in body or spirit heard a new promise of restoration and release, a new time of jubilation.

Paul uses a vivid metaphor to describe the way the Christian community continues the mission of being "God inside out." The Spirit, as love in mission, creates unity and harmony within the very diverse body, where the many parts are all unique, precious, and equally important. The mission is especially focused on attending to those members who are the most vulnerable. As within the divine being, so within the united community of believers: every joy felt by one is shared by all, and every suffering is borne by all.

PRAYING WITH SCRIPTURE

1. How does your faith community reveal "God inside out"?

2. How does the Spirit counter any sense of inferiority or superiority in the exercise of the gifts for mission?

FULFILLED IN OUR HEARING

Fourth Sunday in Ordinary Time

Readings: Jer 1:4-5, 17-19; Ps 71:1-2, 3-4,
5-6, 15, 17; 1 Cor 12:31–13:13; Luke 4:21-30

"Do here in your native place
the things that we heard were done in Capernaum" (Luke 4:23)

Some people know what they want to be when they grow up from the time they are very young. Others discover their vocation as young adults. Still others never seem to find their real mission in life. Jeremiah apparently knew as a very young man what were God's designs for him. Not only did Jeremiah perceive his calling very early but he also understood that it was not something he dreamed up on his own. Rather, it was God, who appointed him as prophet before he was even formed in his mother's womb. Similarly, Luke began his account with the annunciation to Jesus' mother of her child's prophetic mission even before he is conceived in her womb. One can always resist such a calling, especially since prophets always experience suffering in carrying out their mission. People who are lifted up by the prophet's liberating words react with enthusiastic welcome. But for those whose power, privilege, or status is threatened by the prophet's challenges to live justly, the reaction can become even murderous. To Jeremiah, God gives assurance of divine strength to withstand whatever opposition he experiences. Similarly, when the crowd in Nazareth turns on Jesus, he is given the strength to pass unharmed through their midst.

Today's gospel picks up from last Sunday's, in which Jesus first announced his mission to reveal God's liberating and re-creating Spirit through healing and freeing any who were bound. Jesus' neighbors and friends are familiar with the passage from Isaiah that he quotes. At first they marvel when he says that it is fulfilled in their hearing. Jesus, as if reading their thoughts, exposes what is on their minds: "Let's see what you can do." These thoughts seem very close to what the devil says to Jesus in the previous gospel episode. They want him to do a flashy miracle to show off his powers to cure. Instead, Jesus retells stories with which they are well acquainted, stories about earlier prophets who used their healing powers to cure foreign outsiders.

What kind of response is that? One of the implications of Jesus' answer is that the mission he has embraced is, in some ways, not a new one. God's healing Spirit has been revealing the divine intent to heal, restore, and bring all inside into God's loving embrace, even beyond the reach of those to whom God has revealed the law. What is new is the way the Spirit is now embodied in Jesus to bring this revelation to completion.

What Jesus' audience may not have liked is that he is also inviting them to participate in this same saving mission. Jesus' powerful words and deeds are not just something to watch and by which to be impressed. Rather, his mission of jubilee justice is to be taken up and continued by all who hear. Thus it is fulfilled today in our hearing.

PRAYING WITH SCRIPTURE

1. Pray with gratitude for having been called to mission, at whatever stage of your life you accepted it.

2. How does the sense of being called by God fortify you for the difficulties involved in following Jesus?

SEIZED BY GRACE

Fifth Sunday in Ordinary Time

Readings: Isa 6:1-2a, 3-8;
Ps 138:1-2, 2-3, 4-5, 7-8; 1 Cor 15:1-11; Luke 5:1-11

"[B]y the grace of God I am what I am" (1 Cor 15:10)

It can happen anywhere, anytime, to anyone. For Isaiah it was during a religious service in the temple, wrapped in incense and awe-inspiring ritual. For certain Galilean fishermen it was when they were going about their normal, everyday lives, casting and catching, cleaning and communing. With Paul, it was when he was in an angry turmoil, dead set against the new movement of Jesus-followers, determined to keep them from ruining the tradition. The call to mission accompanied by God's transforming grace can strike at any moment.

What always happens when one experiences a call from God is that the immensity of the divine holiness is overpowering. In the face of God's unparalleled goodness, graciousness, and mercy, our own inadequacies and sinfulness loom all the more large. "Woe is me, I am doomed! For I am a man of unclean lips, living among a people of unclean lips," exclaims Isaiah (6:5). "Depart from me, Lord, for I am a sinful man," implores Peter (Luke 5:8). "I am . . . not fit to be called an apostle," insists Paul (1 Cor 15:9). God, however, is never deterred by such protestations. The mission is never dependent upon the worthiness of the minister but upon God's grace. If people kept their focus on their own inabilities and shortcomings, the work of God would never be accomplished. It is when Isaiah lets the seraphim direct his attention away from his unworthiness and toward God's holiness that he then experiences the purging of his sin and the interior freedom to say, "Here I am . . . send me!" (Isa 6:8). When Peter lets go of his certainty that nothing can be caught and relinquishes his fear at what Jesus is asking of him, then he can let himself be seized by grace to bring all his skills to be employed in Jesus' mission.

When Paul accepts that it is by the grace of God that he is what he is, and when he surrenders all that he is to God's power, then he can say that God's "grace to me has not been ineffective" (1 Cor 15:10). The effectiveness of this amazing grace is evident not only in the personal transformation each one experiences but also in the sharing of that transformative power with all who are open to hear.

When one is seized by grace, the gifts and skills one already has are often put to a different use under Christ's direction. One can imagine Peter's reluctance to follow Jesus' suggestion to put out into the deep water, when he and his companions had been hard at it all night without any reward. Why should pros like them listen to Jesus? It is when they can take the sage advice of trying things a different way under Jesus' direction that the grace comes.

While the story of the call of the women disciples, Mary Magdalene, Joanna, Susanna, and their companions (Luke 8:1-3) is not preserved in the New Testament, one can speculate about the ways in which they had to reorient their lives, as they channeled their money and other resources to the Jesus movement. What obstacles would they have had to overcome, such as disapproval by spouses, family, and friends, to dedicate their resources to the Christian mission? These obstacles were no match for the power of grace within them.

PRAYING WITH SCRIPTURE

1. How and when have you been seized by grace?

2. How have you shared that experience so that it unleashes this grace in others?

BLESSED NOW

┌─────────────── **Sixth Sunday in Ordinary Time**

Readings: Jer 17:5-8;
Ps 1:1-2, 3, 4, 6; 1 Cor 15:12, 16-20; Luke 6:17, 20-26
└

"Blessed are you who are poor, / for the kingdom of God is yours" (Luke 6:20)

About 1.4 billion people in the world live on $1.25 or less per day. The majority of poor people worldwide are women. Their opportunities for education are fewer and their earnings still lag far behind those of their male counterparts. Care of home and children go uncompensated. Violence at the hands of their intimate partners costs women in the United States approximately eight million days of work each year, and domestic violence keeps women teetering on the brink of homelessness. How can it be that Jesus would pronounce blessed those who struggle against such poverty?

Biblical scholars point out that the Greek word *makarios*, like the Hebrew *'ashrê*, meaning "blessed," does not confer blessing but recognizes an existing state of happiness. This happiness is something inherent in God and when humans experience blessedness, it flows from relationship with God. In biblical tradition, poverty is never an indicator of blessedness; it is always regarded as evil. What can Jesus mean by stating the opposite?

In the Gospel of Luke, references to the poor are very frequent. Scholars estimate that 25 percent of people in Roman Palestine were desperately poor. Two concrete individual characters put faces on this mass of struggling humanity: the ulcer-ridden beggar Lazarus, lying at the rich man's gate (16:19-31), and the widow who put "her whole life," two small coins, into the temple treasury (21:1-4).

Whenever Jesus speaks about such people, however, he addresses his words to disciples who are not among the most destitute. They are the ones who have the means to be agents of divine blessing to those who are needy. His invitation to disciples is to embrace some form of being poor, but not destitution, as an essential aspect of their commitment to Jesus. Luke shows many options for how to respond to this call to embrace poverty. Some of the fishermen and a tax collector leave behind everything to follow Jesus (5:11, 28). Others, like Zacchaeus, give half their possessions to the poor (19:8). Many of the women put their monetary resources at the service of Jesus' mission (8:1-3). Some, like Mary, the mother of John Mark, opened their homes for the gatherings of the community (Acts 12:12). There was also the practice of pooling everyone's resources and then each taking according to their need (Acts 2:44; 4:32). The only thing that was not an option was to hoard for oneself, like the rich ruler (Luke 18:18-30), or to lie to the community about one's possessions, as the tragic story of Ananias and Sapphira shows (Acts 5:1-11).

The blessedness that Jesus holds up is the happiness of those who are being liberated from their desperate poverty already in the here and now, a foretaste of the final elimination of all want in the fullness of the reign of God. It is not a wish for future reward for an abstract, unknown group of "the poor" who suffer in the present, but a concrete possibility when the needs of real people are known and the resources are shared in community. Remarkably, the word "poor" does not occur in the Acts of the Apostles, where the inequities are being dissolved in the community of believers.

As Lent begins this week, it is a good time to renew our efforts at becoming agents of blessedness through our prayer for those who are in need, fasting in solidarity with those who are hungry not by choice, and almsgiving to those who are destitute.

PRAYING WITH SCRIPTURE

1. How do you embrace a way of being poor for the sake of those who are poor not by choice?

2. How does trust in God become manifest through trust within the community of believers?

GOOD MEASURE

*"[A] good measure, packed together, shaken down, and overflowing,
will be poured into your lap. For the measure with which you measure will
in return be measured out to you"* (Luke 6:38)

The expression "you have to learn to give as good as you get" in American idiom refers to the ability to hold your own in a group of strong-willed people. Sometimes parents say it to their children to encourage them to stand up to bullies. What "you get" is thought to be something challenging or difficult. In today's gospel, the meaning is just the opposite. What we get from the Divine Giver is overflowing abundance of compassion, pardon, and love. Among a people who struggled for enough food, to be given an overflowing measure of grain is an image of the Creator's care and providence. How is one to respond to the unearned gift of God's gracious mercy? The gospel gives the answer: by emulating the One whose child we are.

Jesus spells out some of the ways that God's children do as God does: loving enemies, doing good to those who do hateful things, blessing those who speak abusively, and praying for such people. This manner of acting is not unique to Jesus. The first reading also gives an example of how not to retaliate evil for evil. David chooses not to harm Saul, even though King Saul had been trying to kill David.

Beyond individual actions of nonretaliation, Jesus invites his followers into a fundamental stance in life that must be chosen so that we reflect the image of the One who made us. By continually opening ourselves to the immeasurable goodness, compassion, and love of the Most High, our puny capacities are stretched and expanded. The more we become conscious of how much we graciously receive, the more our measure for giving to others increases.

Such a life stance demands relinquishing what is our more natural re-action: to want to return in kind what we get. If someone strikes us, our instinct is to hit back. If someone speaks unkindly of us, our urge is to match the ugly words with even more hurtful ones toward the other. If something is taken from us, we want repayment with interest. Measure for measure, and then some—that is what we instinctively seek. But Jesus points out that when evil is returned for evil, all it does is increase the measure of evil in the world. Meting out goodness, compassion, pardon, especially when that is contrary to what is directed toward us, subdues and transforms evil. It ruptures the power of evil, and redirects energies toward filling the world with gracious mercy.

This manner of being is not something we are able to accomplish on our own. In the second reading today, Paul speaks about how we are like the first human being in our frailty and corruptibility. But we are also fashioned in the image of the "last Adam," the risen Christ, whose life-giving Spirit does its work of transformation in us, so that our capacity to receive and give love grows to immeasurable proportions.

The final verses in the gospel may at first seem to say that we will be treated by God the way we treat others. But the two previous verses (vv. 35 and 36) give us as the starting point God's unearned goodness and mercy toward us. What enables us to be compassionate, nonjudgmental, forgiving, and giving is that God has first been that way with us. Such divine action in us then shapes our ability to measure the way God does.

PRAYING WITH SCRIPTURE

1. Pray with gratitude for God's immeasurable goodness and love toward you.

2. Ask the Spirit to expand your ability to mete out compassion and love to those who do not treat you with such.

3. Ask Jesus to help you forgive someone who has hurt you.

GRACED SPEECH

Eighth Sunday in Ordinary Time

Readings: Sir 27:4-7;
Ps 92:2-3, 13-14, 15-16; 1 Cor 15:54-58; Luke 6:39-45

"[F]rom the fullness of the heart the mouth speaks" (Luke 6:45)

The most moving homily I ever heard was at a Mass with young Catholics who had a variety of physical disabilities. It was given by a young woman with cerebral palsy. The message was straightforward and simple: "God loves you. God loves me. God loves everybody. We have to love everybody too." Three times she repeated this message, as she turned to each side of the gathered assembly. She beamed as she struggled to get out the words and looked earnestly at every person in the group to be sure they understood. There was no doubt in anyone's mind that she passionately believed this profound message, and that her words came straight from her heart.

Both the first reading and the gospel today offer proverbs and admonitions, several of which center on how a person's speech reveals their inner nature. A bad tree does not bear good fruit, nor does a good tree yield bad produce. Only one with a good heart, centered on God, can speak as did the young preacher who so moved me.

The readings today prompt us to reflect on the care that is needed in speaking. In an age where public discourse, particularly during election season, often degenerates into name-calling, spinning false accusations, and impugning the character of others, a person of faith stands out by his or her refusal to speak ill of others. Moreover, the gospel warns that one who is blind to the goodness in others, and who speaks evil of them instead, reveals his or her own puny measure of openness to God's goodness. Those who see only their neighbors' tiny faults and rush to point those out expose the logjam that blocks their own hearts from receiving and giving God's unfathomable love. A starting point toward transformation of the heart that results in kind words can be vigilance over what one says, curbing the impulse to speak ill of another. That is only a beginning. The gospel envisions a point where the faithful disciple reaches maturity in cultivating inner goodness to such an extent that only good and kind speech would well up from within and pass through the lips.

The first reading notes that it is particularly in adversity that the inner disposition is revealed: "When a sieve is shaken, the husks appear." Anyone can speak well of others when all is going smoothly. But those who can resist returning insult for insult when others speak harshly or make false accusations show their inner mettle refined in tribulation. Like pottery that has passed through the fiery kiln, they emerge stronger, as their inner goodness is shaped to reflect all the more fully that of their Maker.

The power to be transformed in this way, as the second reading reminds us, comes from the One who has passed through the crucible of death, thus overcoming all sin and evil. "God loves you. God loves me. God loves everybody. We have to love everybody too." This is a pretty good summary of all that Christ said and did. What more would one want to say?

PRAYING WITH SCRIPTURE

1. Pray for the gift of inner goodness that comes forth in gracious speech.

2. Ask the Spirit to help you see and affirm the goodness of others, rather than point out their specks of imperfection.

3. Pray for malleability in the hands of the Divine Potter.

WORTHINESS

Ninth Sunday in Ordinary Time

Readings: 1 Kgs 8:41-43;
Ps 117:1, 2; Gal 1:1-2, 6-10; Luke 7:1-10

"He is worthy of having you do this for him" (Luke 7:4, NRSV)

"Lord, I am not worthy that you should enter under my roof, but only say the word and my soul shall be healed." These words from the new Roman Missal that are recited just before Communion at our eucharistic liturgies are based on today's gospel. This is what the centurion's friends are sent to say to Jesus when Jesus is en route to Capernaum to heal the centurion's servant. The story gives us an interesting glimpse into the power relations in occupied Palestine of the first century.

The centurion is a Gentile soldier in the employ of the Roman occupiers, and he commands one hundred soldiers. It is notable that his relationship with the people of the land is a very favorable one. There is mutual benefit: the centurion serves as a patron, obtaining favors and benefits for the people; they in turn offer their services to him in various ways. In a culture of reciprocity, such as this, favors are done in order to secure a return benefit. Saving up favor with a powerful patron is important so that one can call in a favor when there is a serious need. The centurion has a highly valued slave who is near death, and he calls on his clients to make his case for him to Jesus. The Jewish elders serve as go-betweens, telling Jesus that the centurion "loves our people," and give as evidence that he has secured funds for the building of their synagogue. They assure Jesus that for this reason, he is worthy of the favor he is requesting.

In the world of patrons, clients, and their brokers, this interaction makes perfect sense. But in divine interactions with people, worthiness is not a factor. Nothing that human beings do earns God's favor—it is a free, boundless gift given. Divine favor does not operate according to the expectations of reciprocity and merit. It is accepted by believers through faith, but it can never be fully reciprocated in kind.

In its most startling manifestation, those acting in the manner of the Divine Patron exhibit unmerited graciousness toward those who are outsiders. If the centurion was sensitive to Jesus' incurring of ritual impurity if he came into his home, Jesus instead invites the centurion into his abode, that is, his family of faith. So we too, when we gather as Jesus' family under his roof, express our faith in his gift of himself, with gratitude for the immense gratuity of this exchange. It is not a prayer of groveling self-deprecation we pray before Communion, but rather one in which we voice our acceptance of this unearned gift, allowing it to feed our faith and to manifest itself in our gracious and loving acts toward others.

This is a much more difficult pattern of gift exchange to put into practice than that of equal return of favor for favor. Paul discovers how easy it is for a people to revert to a way of trying to earn divine favor after having first accepted his preaching of the gospel of Christ's free gift of himself. In his letter to the Galatians, Paul insists that there is no other kind of good news; one cannot merit God's gifts through keeping the law, as some might tell them.

It is much more demanding to open oneself to the unmerited gift of Christ, allowing him to bring healing and wholeness both to oneself and to all the precious daughters and sons whom he has drawn under his roof.

PRAYING WITH SCRIPTURE

1. Ask Jesus to help you let go of any desire to earn his love.

2. Are there any persons you'd rather not be with under the same roof? Listen to what Jesus might say.

GIVEN INTO OUR MOTHER'S ARMS

Tenth Sunday in Ordinary Time

Readings: 1 Kgs 17:17-24; Ps 30:2, 4, 5-6, 11, 12, 13; Gal 1:11-19; Luke 7:11-17

"The dead man sat up and began to speak,
and Jesus gave him to his mother" (Luke 7:15)

The Madres de la Plaza de Mayo still stand weekly in front of the *Casa Rosada*, the home of the president in Buenos Aires, demanding to know the fate of their husbands, sons, and brothers, who disappeared during Argentina's "dirty war" in the 1970s. They know they cannot bring back to life the thirty thousand *desaparecidos*, but they stand in silent protest to ensure that such senseless deaths never occur again.

In today's readings we see two widows, each of whom mourns the death of her only son. In the first reading, the widow protests aloud to Elijah, to whom she has offered hospitality. She accuses him of helping to bring this calamity upon her. Elijah, in turn, pleads with God, stretches himself upon the child, and the boy is restored to health. In the gospel, the widow does not speak. But Jesus sees her, is filled with compassion, and brings her son back to life. Her tears and her grief might be considered a silent protest against death. Both stories end with the prophet giving the son to his mother: the child does not belong to death, but to the one who gave him life. At the conclusion of both incidents there is an acclamation of recognition that the prophet is one who belongs to God. The widow in Zarephath exclaims, "Now indeed I know that you are a man of God" and in Nain the crowd glorifies God and proclaims that Jesus is God's prophet. Elijah and Jesus belong to the Author of Life and are agents of divine life. By their actions they protest death and all its machinations.

Both these stories are about resuscitation, that is, restoring a person to the earthly life he had enjoyed previously. Both are returned to those who gave them physical birth. Not all mothers who rail against the death of a beloved child have him or her restored in this life. But these episodes give a foretaste of what God does in resurrecting Jesus. Like a mother who loses an only son to death, God takes him back into her arms, not restored to earthly life, but to live forever in the divine embrace. God does this not only for Jesus but also for every beloved daughter and son, each one as precious as if an only child. And once all the daughters and sons are raised up, there will be no more bereaved parents, as all are alive again, given into the arms of their true mother.

This profound journey of transformation is already begun in this life, each time we allow ourselves to be opened up to the power of God to turn us away from deadly choices. In the second reading, Paul speaks of one of the most dramatic moments in his journey when he was turned away from his death-dealing persecution of the fledgling church. He comes to know that the one who had fashioned him and set him apart before he was born has called him to lead the way in engendering faith among the Gentiles. This revelation is an extraordinary resuscitation for both Paul and the fledgling church.

Every time we, like Paul, Elijah, Jesus, and the mothers who protest the deaths of their children, allow God's life-giving force to fill us, direct us, change us, and urge us forward to protest senseless and preventable deaths in any way we can, we are already tasting resurrected life.

PRAYING WITH SCRIPTURE

1. How have you experienced being raised to life?

2. How do you protest senseless deaths?

3. Let yourself be given into the arms of Mother God.

GREAT FORGIVENESS, GREAT LOVE

> **Eleventh Sunday in Ordinary Time**
>
> *Readings:* 2 Sam 12:7-10, 13;
> Ps 32:1-2, 5, 7, 11; Gal 2:16, 19-21; Luke 7:36–8:3

"[H]er many sins have been forgiven;
hence, she has shown great love" (Luke 7:47, NABRE)

How do you make amends when you know you have hurt someone deeply or when you become aware that your patterns of life choices cause great harm to others? Sometimes you can kiss and make up with the hurt person. But at other times it is not possible to repair the damage to the ones directly affected. Even as remorse and relief flood over you when you become the recipient of forgiveness, you search for how to express the love and joy that come from being freed from guilt. Today's gospel captures a scene in which a woman who had been known as a sinner, and who had experienced forgiveness, pours out her joy and gratitude toward Jesus in lavish demonstrations of love.

The rest of the woman's story is lost to us. We do not know her name or from where she came or any other details of her life. We do not know what kinds of sins she had committed, or how she met Jesus. We do not know when or where it was that he had absolved her from her sins (the tense of the verb *apheōntai*, "have been forgiven," in verse 47 indicates an action that happened in the past whose effect endures into the present). We have only one small slice of her life, a moment in which she takes advantage of the open door for poor people to partake of the scraps of a banquet, and she enters the home of Simon to seek out the One whose kindness and love had set her free. She finds the guests reclining on cushions, reaching into the center to partake of the food, with their feet extending out into the room. She spots Jesus, and in an extravagant gesture of love, she mingles her tears of joy with precious perfume, and anoints his feet.

This act is open to misinterpretation. Simon, the host, immediately harbors judgmental thoughts. He is certain in his knowledge that the woman is a sinner, and he is unaware of the forgiveness she has experienced. He is just as certain in his judgment of Jesus: he cannot be a prophet. Much as the prophet Nathan used a parable to bring King David to repent of his murder of Uriah (see the verses immediately preceding today's first reading), Jesus tells Simon a parable aimed at getting him to repent of his false judgment and to open himself to the forgiveness Jesus offers.

The point of the parable is easy to grasp: great love flows from having been forgiven much. While Simon easily grasps this in story form, we are left to wonder if he got the point when Jesus brings his attention back to real life and asks him to look again at the woman. Jesus retells what he saw: great gestures of love outpoured that sprang from having received great forgiveness. He contrasts her great capacity for forgiveness and love with Simon's puny capacity and invites the Pharisee into this expansive love. As the story ends we do not know how Simon responded. Did he accept Jesus' offer, or did he join his table companions in murmuring critically about Jesus' ability to forgive? The story turns the question toward us as well: How do we perceive forgiven sinners? How do we ourselves respond to Jesus' offer of forgiveness and love?

The scene that follows provides an exemplary response. Having been healed of severe illness, Mary Magdalene, Joanna, Susanna, and other Galilean women expend all their monetary resources (this is the connotation of the Greek word *hyparchontōn*) for Jesus and his mission.

PRAYING WITH SCRIPTURE

1. Ask Jesus to expand your capacity to receive forgiveness.

2. How have you been freed so as to extend lavish love to others?

3. Ask for the grace to suspend judgment and to perceive grace at work in others.

CLOTHED IN CHRIST

Twelfth Sunday in Ordinary Time

Readings: Zech 12:10-11; 13:1;
Ps 63:2, 3-4, 5-6, 8-9; Gal 3:26-29; Luke 9:18-24

*"For all of you who were baptized into Christ
have clothed yourselves with Christ"* (Gal 3:27)

Arriving at church a few Sundays ago was a family all bedecked in their very finest, carrying a tiny infant, engulfed in a long white gown, a miniature version of the white robe given to newly baptized adults at the Easter Vigil. The symbolism of the gown was perfect: the child who was "putting on Christ" was completely covered with the flowing fabric. It was even impossible to distinguish whether the child was a boy or a girl.

The famous verses from Paul's Letter to the Galatians in today's second reading were likely words taken from an early Christian baptismal formula. They make the extraordinary assertion that when we are clothed with Christ in baptism, the status markers that determine our place in society exist no longer. Within a religious movement that was born amid the Jewish people and that was attracting an increasing number of Gentiles, Paul asserts that baptism in Christ gives all equal status in the family of God—all are descendants of Abraham and Sarah, all are children of God, and all are equal heirs. There is no privilege accorded to those who were the firstborn. Nor are there different levels of inheritance; all are one and equal in Christ.

A second determination of status is also eclipsed: the demarcations between freeborn, freed, and slave are dissolved in the waters of baptism. Finally, in a world in which males held all the power to make decisions and in which women were to be subordinate to men, baptism erased distinction in status based on gender. This is an extraordinary assertion of egalitarianism.

It is most likely, however, that Paul is referring to equality of all Christians in terms of their salvation, not necessarily as something to be enacted in the social structures of his day. In other letters, he advises believers not to change status. He instructs the Corinthians, for example, that those who were uncircumcised should remain so and that slaves should stay slaves (1 Cor 7:17-24). One of the reasons for this advice was that Paul believed the Parousia, the Second Coming, was imminent.

Two millennia later, with a heightened sense of global human rights and a vast tradition of social justice in the church, the question of incorporating this baptismal vision of equal status in social and ecclesial structures takes on a different urgency. Baptism does not wash away the differences, but it makes them irrelevant. All who are clothed with Christ belong equally and have equal status. Just as the white gown masked the tiny babe's gender, so does baptism cover over any status markers in communities of equal disciples.

The ending of today's gospel moves in a similar direction, as Jesus asks his followers to deny themselves and take up their cross daily. In one sense, baptism is the first step in a lifelong effort to let go of any desire for privilege based on status. This "denial of self" is a daily search for the common good, and requires relinquishment of self-aggrandizement on the part of those who have power, privilege, or status. For those whose circumstances of birth or misfortune place them at the underside of society, the movement is one of empowerment instead of relinquishment, as with the Anointed One, who saves life by losing his own.

No structures that thrive on inequality are brought down easily. Jesus knew this and tried to prepare his disciples for the conflagration that would cost him his life. The question still confronts us: Are we also willing to take up this same struggle each day, clothed in the power of the One who has gone before us through death to new life?

PRAYING WITH SCRIPTURE

1. Pray with the image of yourself as "clothed in Christ."

2. Pray to see all others as also "clothed in Christ."

3. Ask the Spirit to strengthen you in your struggle for the baptismal equality Paul envisions.

THE PATH TO LIFE

Thirteenth Sunday in Ordinary Time

Readings: 1 Kgs 19:16b, 19-21;
Ps 16:1-2, 5, 7-8, 9-10, 11; Gal 5:1, 13-18; Luke 9:51-62

"I will follow you wherever you go" (Luke 9:57)

The threats from the loggers and ranchers and their hired gunmen were coming more frequently. Some urged her to leave or to desist her relentless outcry against the devastation of the Brazilian rainforest. But Sr. Dorothy Stang, SND, would not leave the poor farmers whose homes and livelihood were in peril. She forged on through almost impassable muddy roads to reach them, to read the Scriptures and pray together, to bolster their courage to stand up against injustice, and to urge them to live in harmony with the rainforest, with God, and with one another. Her resolute journey ended when she was gunned down on February 12, 2005.

In today's gospel we see the same resolute determination on the part of Jesus not to deviate from the path on which he had set out, to advocate for life for the most vulnerable. The opposition against him is mounting, and he knows it. He chooses not to turn back. There were still many ancient hatreds that needed healing, one of which was the enmity between his people and Samaritans. He tries to meet them in their own territory, but they will not receive him. The infuriated disciples want to do as Elijah did (2 Kgs 1:10) and call down on them fire from heaven. Jesus instead urged them to peaceably journey on to another village with him.

En route Jesus encounters three potential followers. Many commentators understand these as people who are initially enthusiastic but are not able to embrace the serious demands of discipleship once Jesus articulates these. But each encounter is left open-ended and we are not told whether or not the person does ultimately follow Jesus. They all pose questions to us about our own commitment to follow Jesus all the way to Jerusalem.

The first person approaches Jesus, expressing a desire to follow him. With words akin to Ruth's profession of loyalty to Naomi (Ruth 1:16), the first says, "I will follow you wherever you go." This potential disciple rightly voices that following Jesus requires wholehearted dedication to him. In reply Jesus warns that his is an itinerant mission that demands mobility to go where the needs are and a letting go of any possessiveness, even of a bed of one's own.

In the second encounter, Jesus initiates the call to follow. This person wants to take care first of filial obligations to his parents. Jesus invites him to embrace a larger family obligation: to extend his concern for life to all God's family as his kin and to proclaim well-being for all in God's realm.

The third person, like the first, initiates the encounter and expresses a desire to follow Jesus, asking to bid farewell first to his family, as did Elisha when called by Elijah. Jesus warns that any who come with him will not be able to return to what was before. They are forever changed and must proclaim the reign of God. Just as Dorothy Stang could not leave the people she had come to love in her forty years of ministry in the Amazon rainforest, so disciples must follow the path of Jesus until their own moment of being "taken up" in death and resurrection.

We do not know whether the three would-be disciples accepted these sobering challenges and continued on the way with Jesus. If the conditions Jesus sets forth seem daunting, Paul reminds us that this is not a yoke of slavery we take up, but a freeing power to live by the Spirit. Just as Elijah clothed Elisha with the mantle of his prophetic power, so anyone who accepts Jesus' invitation to become a disciple is wrapped in the protective cloak of his spirit, enabling such a one to love even the neighbor whose hatred tries to block the spread of the good news.

PRAYING WITH SCRIPTURE

1. How have you experienced the freedom of life in the Spirit?

2. In what ways have you not been able to "go back home" once you chose to follow Jesus?

3. How do you resist "calling down fire from heaven" on those who oppose God's reign?

LABORERS FOR THE HARVEST

Fourteenth Sunday in Ordinary Time

Readings: Isa 66:10-14c; Ps 66:1-3,
4-5, 6-7, 16, 20; Gal 6:14-18; Luke 10:1-12, 17-20

"The harvest is abundant but the laborers are few" (Luke 10:2)

A recent radio interview featured a journalist who decided to spend a year doing jobs that most Americans will not do. One of these jobs was to harvest lettuce. For two months he was the only white person toiling among Mexican migrant workers. He described the backbreaking labor vividly and how he had to become numb to the pains in his back and hands and arms to make it through each day. He had to ignore his fierce thirst in the relentless heat and sun, for to take a break to get water would put him hopelessly behind.

What was most impressive in his story was the way that people helped one another in the fields. When one person was sick and could not keep up the pace, all the others automatically took on a bit more of a load to help her get through the day. This work is so physically strenuous and the pay so meager that few, if any, would ever aspire to it; migrants desperate for any income take it gladly.

In today's gospel Jesus invites his disciples to take up the very strenuous work of evangelization. As in the lettuce fields, the harvest is abundant, but those who are willing to take on this demanding work are few. Those who do take it up are "like lambs among wolves," gentle and loving, while facing fierce opposition that could even devour them. Like migrant workers in the United States, whose presence is unwanted yet whose work is indispensable, laborers in God's vineyard also face frequent rejection.

Furthermore, they bring with them no provisions and no defenses. For their food they are dependent on what is offered to them. They deserve payment, but there is no guarantee they will receive it. Like migrants who cannot raise their voice in protest against injustices toward them for fear of deportation, missionaries may need to move to another town, another field, another kind of crop, if there is no welcome for them in the first place they preach. Their vulnerability proclaims an alternative kind of power to that of the reigning systems: God's saving power of love in the crucified Christ. Throughout, they are to be bearers of peace proclaiming God's reign. What would entice anyone to take up such work?

The last part of the gospel points to the rewarding aspects of this difficult work. When proclaimers of the gospel can see that the power they use for good is able to transform evil situations, the ensuing joy is indescribable. It is essential for them, however, not to focus on the visible results of their handiwork and not to take false pride in what they may think has been accomplished by their own efforts. Their true joy comes from acknowledging the divine source of the power they are able to wield, as they entrust themselves fully to the One who has called them to mission.

Like the returning exiles addressed in the first reading, who are filled with rejoicing over the rebuilding of Jerusalem, they know that they rest under God's protective mantle, where they may "suck fully of the milk of her comfort," and "nurse with delight at her abundant breasts." It is the Holy One who will "spread prosperity over Jerusalem like a river," carrying its inhabitants in her arms, fondling them in her lap, "as a mother comforts her child."

Those who respond to Jesus' invitation to go out into the fields never go alone. Like the workers cutting lettuce, they have partners who rally in support of anyone who is flagging, ensuring that none is left behind and that all together share in the joy of a successful harvest.

PRAYING WITH SCRIPTURE

1. What rigors do you face in sharing the gospel with others?

2. How have you experienced joy from being a transformative power for good?

3. Let God's motherly care enfold you as you allow yourself to be formed for mission.

WHAT TO DO

Fifteenth Sunday in Ordinary Time

Readings: Deut 30:10-14; Ps 69:14,
17, 30-31, 33-34, 36, 37; Col 1:15-20; Luke 10:25-37

"[W]hat must I do to inherit eternal life?" (Luke 10:25)

There are all kinds of good reasons for not stopping to help a stranger: I have other pressing obligations. It's dangerous—what if the robbers are still lurking and attack me? I don't have any professional skills or resources to help this person. If I move him and make his injuries worse, he might sue me. And on and on.

I can easily talk myself out of any good deed, just like the scholar of the law in today's gospel. He knew what to do. He knew what his religious convictions prompted him to do. He could recite the law perfectly. He also knew what his heart was urging him to do. He just needed somebody to reassure him that his rationalizations were well founded and that no one would expect him to do anything for some stranger in need.

It would have been easy for Jesus to give him the answer he wanted: "Yes, of course you're right. He is not your responsibility. Someone better equipped will tend to him." But he does not. Jesus knows that it will not be easy for the scholar to hear his answer. Better than rational arguments, a story will help the scholar move out of his head and listen to his heart. There is, however, a twist to the story that Jesus tells. It is not a straightforward tale about someone like the scholar who is "moved with compassion" that he might easily emulate.

The complication is that the scholar of the law would never identify with a hated Samaritan. More likely he would see himself in the person in need at the side of the road. From that perspective, he would watch in horror as the priest and Levite, the ones he would expect to act with pastoral attention, pass him by while justifying themselves. To receive lavish aid from a despised Samaritan breaks open the strictures of his heart, as he experiences a flood of grace from this unexpected source.

The parable asks the scholar, stripped of his defenses, to accept the ways in which divine compassion and grace have been showered upon him undeservedly. From this place, he could then be prompted to extend these to others.

The question is not really "who is my neighbor?" Deep down the scholar knows that each human being and every creature are neighbor and kin, all relying on one another in the fragile web of life. The scholar does not want to admit this to himself because of what it will ask of him. In the depths of his heart, however, he knows what he must do to aid a fellow traveler in need. It is not really too hard or too mysterious to figure out, as Moses tells the Israelites in the first reading. You do not need someone to "go up in the sky" or "cross the sea." How to live out God's way as elaborated in the Scriptures is actually "something very near to you, already in your mouths and in your hearts; you have only to carry it out," as Moses asserts.

Sometimes we need to be helped out of our rationalizations for not doing what our listening heart prompts us to do. At other times we are asked to be the one who can speak truth lovingly to a friend who struggles to do what compassion asks of him or her.

Heeding the voice of God to know what is the right action and the right time requires deep listening, in contemplative silent prayer, in honest conversation with trusted friends and openness to hearing the cacophonous cries of needy neighbors at hand and throughout the globe. We do not know whether the scholar of the law let go of trying to justify himself and was able to "go and do likewise." The parable remains open-ended, inviting us to hear it addressed to ourselves. How will it end?

PRAYING WITH SCRIPTURE

1. What do you do to help you listen to the cries of those in need and to heed the voice of God?

2. When have you experienced compassion and grace from an unexpected source?

3. What does that experience of grace prompt you to do?

A WOMAN'S PLACE

Sixteenth Sunday in Ordinary Time

Readings: Gen 18:1-10a;
Ps 15:2-3, 3-4, 5; Col 1:24-28; Luke 10:38-42

"Martha welcomed him into her home" (Luke 10:38, NRSV)

Martha always gets a bad rap. In traditional interpretations of her story she is said to be too preoccupied or anxious about the details of hospitality to attend well to her guest. Her sister, by contrast, sits in rapt attention at Jesus' feet, drinking in his every word. When Jesus declares that it is Mary who has "chosen the better part," the message we are supposed to take away, according to many commentators, is that contemplation rather than active service is the harder but better choice, and that no one can minister without first sitting and learning at Jesus' feet. While finding the right balance between contemplation and action is a perennial challenge for most Christians, that may not actually be the question that today's gospel addresses. There are many tensions in the story left unanswered by the traditional interpretation.

Recently New Testament scholars have proposed that this gospel incident may be more a reflection of the situation of the Lukan communities and the questions they were trying to resolve, rather than a report of an episode in the life of Jesus. They have noticed that what concerns Martha is much *diakonia*, and her distress is over her sister leaving her to carry it out alone. Both the noun *diakonia* and the verb *diakonein* occur in verse 40.

Elsewhere in the New Testament, these terms refer primarily to ministerial service, as in Jesus' declaration of his mission "to serve," not to "be served" (Mark 10:45; Luke 22:27). In New Testament times, *diakonia* covered a wide range of ministries. In the case of Mary Magdalene, Joanna, Susanna, and the other Galilean women who "provided for" Jesus and the itinerant preachers "out of their resources," *diakonein* refers to financial ministry (the Greek word *hyparchontōn* connotes monetary resources; Luke 8:3). This is the same nuance *diakonia* has in Acts 11:29 and 12:25 regarding Paul's collection for Jerusalem. In Acts 6:2 *diakonein* refers to table ministry, while in Acts 6:4 *diakonia* connotes ministry of the word. In Acts 1:25 *diakonia* is apostolic ministry. One individual in the New Testament is named a *diakonos*, Phoebe, "deacon of the church at Cenchreae" (Rom 16:1, NRSV).

Scholars are now thinking that the incident in today's gospel is not about preparing a meal; instead, Martha voices how burdened her heart is over the conflicts surrounding women's exercise of their ministries in the early church. Some people were greatly in favor of women evangelizers and teachers like Prisca (Acts 18:26), Euodia and Syntyche (Phil 4:3); women prophets like Philip's four daughters (Acts 21:9); and women heads of house churches, like Nympha (Col 4:15), Mary (Acts 12:12), Lydia (Acts 16:40), and Prisca (Rom 16:5; 1 Cor 16:19). Others, however, argued that a woman's place was in the home and that speaking and ministering in the public sphere belonged to the men (e.g., 1 Cor 14:34-35; 1 Tim 2:11-12). Luke takes the latter position, giving it validity by placing approval of the silent Mary on Jesus' lips.

There was never any question in the early church about women becoming disciples. Both Martha and Mary welcomed Jesus and the word he spoke (vv. 38-39). The controversy swirled around what women would do with what they learned while sitting at Jesus' feet. The answer Luke gave was quite understandable for his time. Today's gospel invites us to reflect on what answer Jesus might give today to the question of a woman's place in the ministries of the church as they have now evolved.

PRAYING WITH SCRIPTURE

1. How do you foster a spirit of hospitality to receive God's word with openness from whomever comes into your home?

2. How has the word come alive for you through women's ministries?

3. What does "choosing the better part" mean today?

A FORGIVING AND GIVING GOD

Seventeenth Sunday in Ordinary Time

Readings: Gen 18:20-32;
Ps 138:1-2, 2-3, 6-7, 7-8; Col 2:12-14; Luke 11:1-13

*"[H]ow much more will the Father in heaven give . . .
to those who ask him?"* (Luke 11:13)

Some years ago a friend's wife was ill and needed surgery. My friend was terrified, as his wife of thirty years had never been sick. He began bargaining with God. He promised God that if she came through the surgery and recovered, he would give up cigarettes. He quit cold turkey right then and there. She recovered quickly after the surgery and returned to excellent health.

In the gospel today Jesus tells a parable, followed by several sayings, to convey how extraordinarily loving and gracious God is and how greatly God wants to shower us with what is good. We don't have to try to convince God to be generous toward us—that is the very thing God wants to do!

Jesus tells a parable about a person who has a special need late at night, after a guest arrives unexpectedly. He goes to his neighbor to ask for bread to serve to the guest. Even though the neighbor and his family are sound asleep, surely he will respond. In the very unlikely case that the neighbor's care for his friend falters, his sensitivity to the shame that failure to respond would bring on his own household would impel him to open the door and supply the bread. The motive ascribed to the friend making the request in verse 8, *anaideia*, is often rendered "persistence." But the Greek word is more accurately translated "shamelessness."

The sense is that the sleeping friend responds to the request for bread to avoid having shame come upon his household and the village, who all share responsibility for hospitality to the guest. The opening line of the parable asks a rhetorical question that sets up the expected response: It is completely unthinkable that a friend would act shamefully by denying a friend in need. A friend would most certainly give what is asked and more. The point of the parable is that God's response to us when we are needy is like that of the generously giving friend. The translation "persistence" originates from the Latin versions from the fifth century onward that inaccurately rendered *anaideia* as *importunitatem*.

The sayings that follow the parable reinforce its meaning, elaborating that God stands ready and eager to open the door to whoever knocks and to give whatever we ask, just as parents desire to give good gifts to their children.

The gospel challenges the idea that God sends suffering to test or challenge or strengthen us and insists that God desires only good for us. We do not have to badger God or bargain with God to give us good things.

A careful reading of today's first Scripture passage, from Genesis, also reveals God's desire for well-being for all, not a desire to punish from which God must be dissuaded. The text begins with God going to investigate whether the outcry against the people of Sodom and Gomorrah is warranted. The answer to that question is never given in the text. Instead, Abraham begins to bargain with God, taking it for granted that God has made a judgment to sweep away all those who are presumed guilty. Over and over God's response is, "I will not destroy."

In the opening lines of the gospel, Jesus teaches his disciples to pray, showing them how to begin by centering on God's holiness, God's realm, and God's bountiful gifts of daily food and forgiveness. By accepting these unearned and abundant gifts, disciples are transformed into people who are increasingly giving and forgiving, like God. The persistence needed is not to keep imploring God so as to change God's mind, but to keep on faithfully praying so as to be changed into an icon of the divine generosity.

PRAYING WITH SCRIPTURE

1. Begin your prayer today with an extended time of thanksgiving to God for God's immense generosity to you.

2. How do you remain persistent in prayer?

3. How is God transforming you into an icon of divine generosity?

BIGGER BARNS

Eighteenth Sunday in Ordinary Time

Readings: Eccl 1:2; 2:21-23;
Ps 90:3-4, 5-6, 12-13; Col 3:1-5, 9-11; Luke 12:13-21

"Put to death . . . the greed that is idolatry" (Col 3:5)

For me, it's books. I just cannot get enough. Not only are there new ones that I always want to read, but I want to acquire my own copies. And I never let them go. You never know when you are going to want to reread or consult them again. And so I need more and more bookshelves. But, where is the boundary between legitimate need for books (or whatever we are tempted to accumulate) for ministry and pleasure, and greedy acquisition?

The gospel today shows us in parable form what the "greed that is idolatry" looks like. The author of Colossians urges us to "put to death" this vice as we "put on the new self" that is Christ. In the Scriptures, there are many texts that underscore that having riches is not sinful; it is what one does with them that determines virtue or vice. Abraham, for example, was said to be highly favored by God, because he had great flocks and herds, a large family, and a great number of servants (Gen 13:2; 26:13-14).

In the gospel story, however, the rich man with the bountiful harvest is shown to be isolated, oblivious of both God and his fellow human beings. His soliloquy reveals his self-centeredness. Rather than consult those whose lives are intertwined with his, he asks himself, "What shall I do . . . I do not have space . . . I shall do . . . I shall tear down . . . I shall store . . . I shall say to myself . . ." The focus of his reflection is "my harvest . . . my barns . . . my grain . . . myself."

In a world of limited goods, his solution is shocking: he will tear down his barns and build bigger ones, where he will stockpile his goods for many years. First-century Palestinians did not operate within a system of capitalism. There was no expectation that all could keep getting richer. They considered all goods limited, so that if one person acquired more, it necessarily meant that others went without. Hoarding, for them, was a clear sign of greed, the vice most destructive to community life.

The rich man's self-centered plan for stockpiling and spending for his own enjoyment is interrupted by a startling apparition by God, the only such divine intervention in a gospel parable. "You fool" comes the accusation, with the notice that this very night his "life will be demanded." The critical question is: All "the things you have prepared, to whom will they belong?" The clear biblical answer comes from Psalm 24:1: "The earth is the Lord's and all it holds, the world and those who dwell in it" (NABRE). Everything belongs to God; even life itself is given to us on loan. In the end the greedy man has no benefit from all he has acquired, and his heirs will be left haggling over it.

The parable also hints at how the miserly man will meet his end. If Jesus was addressing this parable to poor peasants, whose backbreaking labor did not result to their own benefit but only increased the riches of the landowner, their answer to the question of ownership would have a different ring. Would not the land and its fruits, which come from their toil, belong to them? Is it the peasant workers who, in an uprising, are demanding the life of the rich man?

The parable cuts two ways: to those who are blessed with abundance, hard questions are posed about legitimate use, greediness, and just distribution of resources for the common good. To those on the underside of privilege, there is encouragement to take action to unmask vicious greed and to engage in efforts to bring about economic justice, while heeding an implicit warning that violence and killing are futile means for achieving just ends.

PRAYING WITH SCRIPTURE

1. Pray with gratitude for the gift of life and all that you have on loan.

2. How does the parable speak to you about just distribution of goods in our modern world?

3. How might your faith community discern together what to do?

OBEDIENT FAITH

Nineteenth Sunday in Ordinary Time

Readings: Wis 18:6-9; Ps 33:1,
12, 18-19, 20-22; Heb 11:1-2, 8-19; Luke 12:32-48

"By faith Abraham obeyed" (Heb 11:8)

In a rural village in Chiapas, Mexico, an indigenous woman reflects, "My whole life I was taught to obey. First of all, I obeyed my father and mother. At age twelve my father decided whom I would marry. My father and his father made the agreement. I had no say. I could not object that I didn't even know the man to whom my father had promised me. My only choice was to do my father's will."

"My father and mother told me this: Obey the commands of your father-in-law and your mother-in-law and your husband. You will only be happy if you obey. After I was married I tried to obey my husband in everything. He was the one who always made the decisions. I tried to be an obedient daughter and wife, but my father was wrong. I was not happy. My heart was always sad. I would cry out to God in my prayers, but the only answer I got was that God ordained that it should be this way."

This woman's story, along with the stories of others like her, is shared in the book *Con Mirada, Mente y Corazon de Mujer* (Mexico D.F.: CODIMUJ, 1999). She, through the sharing of Scripture with other women who have learned how to read "with the eyes, mind, and heart of a woman," discovered a new meaning of obedience that took her far beyond her initial understanding. In this she is like Abraham and Sarah, as described in the second reading, and like Peter and the other disciples in the gospel.

The reading from Hebrews emphasizes how obedience flows from faith in a trustworthy God. It elaborates how Abraham obeyed the call from God to go out from the place he knew, "not knowing where he was to go." All he and Sarah had to go on was God's promise and their experience of generative power that was given to them by God. They set out obediently in faith, because everything they had experienced of God's gracious goodness led them to trust the Holy One for whatever lay ahead.

The gospel outlines how one becomes disposed to hear, to know, and to act on God's will. First, one must let go of fear so as to be able to receive the gift of God's kingdom. This is God's great joy: to find us unafraid and delighting in this indescribable gift. Obedience out of fear of a punishing God has no place among Jesus' followers. Rather, obedience is the single-hearted response in faith to the One who is love incarnate and who frees us to love in like manner.

Freeing the heart from attachment to anything but God's love and God's realm is the next step in obedience. Selling belongings and giving alms ensures that possessions do not become the treasure that grips the heart. Also needed is a sharpening of the senses, watching intently for all signs of divine presence and directives, through vigilance in prayer and attentiveness to the hungers of our world. Finally, when the master becomes the servant, there is a dismantling of systems wherein some are masters and others servants. The meaning of this parable comes clear in the Last Supper scene, where it is enacted by Jesus himself.

Obedient faith that dismantles unjust master/servant dichotomies is not an easy road, as women from the Bible study groups in Chiapas attest: "At first we felt guilty, we thought we were disobeying the law of God. It's been a long process, but we kept talking and listening to one another. Now we know that it is not God who commands it to be so, but it is a matter of culture and education. We were not born to be subservient as we had been made to believe, but to be obedient to God, who wants us to be happy."

PRAYING WITH SCRIPTURE

1. How does contemplation and listening to the hungers of the world help you to discern God's will?

2. Enjoy God's delight in giving us the kingdom.

3. How does obedience in faith undermine subservience?

UNWANTED MESSENGERS

Twentieth Sunday in Ordinary Time

Readings: Jer 38:4-6,
8-10; Ps 40:2, 3, 4, 18; Heb 12:1-4; Luke 12:49-53

"Do you think that I have come to establish peace on the earth?" (Luke 12:51)

There's something in us that resists hearing messages of doom. There's no such thing as global warming, some will say. The Holocaust is a hoax; it never happened, some insist. If we accepted what those attuned to Earth are telling us, it would demand that we make difficult changes in our patterns of consumption of Earth's resources. If we learn about how racism can lead to genocide, it would ask us to confront racist attitudes in ourselves and in our nation, and would demand that we embrace new patterns of relating. But nobody likes hearing prophets who speak the truth about dire consequences that will befall us unless we change.

One way to shut out the voice of an unwanted prophet is to try to do away with her or him. In the first reading, the officials are able to convince the king that Jeremiah is not seeking the good of the people but its harm. He is "weakening the hands" of the soldiers and needlessly worrying the people with his warnings about the impending fall of Jerusalem (my translation). The officials are able to persuade King Zedekiah to give Jeremiah into their hands. They throw him into a cistern, where they leave him to die, until a eunuch in the king's house persuades the king to order his rescue.

We see a kind of tug of war in the first reading. Some heed the prophet's words and welcome his warning, while others resist the threat to their power, privilege, and status that Jeremiah's message poses. Jesus speaks of the same kind of divided reaction that his ministry provokes. As he ignites in his followers a vision of justice, peace, and well-being for all that could blaze forth, some readily welcome it. Others resist it mightily. The resisters are not eager for the burning away of their comforts and privileges as Jesus' way of transformation demands. The divisions over Jesus' message reach even into the inner recesses of the home, pitting family members against one another, as they struggle with what the gospel demands of them and how to heed it. Like King Zedekiah, who listens first to one set of officials, and then to a servant with a different perspective, Christians are confronted with differing interpretations of what the gospel demands. It is easy to reject the version of a prophet that insists on transformative change. Better to get rid of such an unwelcome messenger and continue on undisturbed.

Jesus warns his followers not to be taken by surprise if his message provokes conflict and division. The way toward genuine peace is not a gentle, easy road. It is a path that entails struggle. Injustice does not die without heavy resistance. Those who embark on Jesus' way, however, are empowered by their baptism. Baptism brings both refreshment and joy from being washed of sin, as well as an induction into a difficult lifelong burning away of anything within that stands opposed to the gospel. Inflamed with the power of the Spirit, those baptized in Christ are empowered to continue his mission of healing divisions, as diverse hearts and minds are fused into one in the furnace of Christ's love.

PRAYING WITH SCRIPTURE

1. What messages of contemporary prophets do you find yourself resisting?

2. How are obstacles to deeper gospel living being burned away in you?

3. How does the Spirit empower you for Christ's reconciling work?

SPIRITUAL TRAINING

Twenty-First Sunday in Ordinary Time

Readings: Isa 66:18-21;
Ps 117:1, 2; Heb 12:5-7, 11-13; Luke 13:22-30

"Strive to enter through the narrow gate" (Luke 13:24)

Jesus often does not give straight answers to questions posed to him. Today's gospel story, for instance, starts with someone asking him, "will only a few people be saved?" It seems like a straightforward question about numbers. But Jesus perceives that the questioner and the others whom he was teaching were not really as concerned about the final head count as they were about whether they themselves would be included among the redeemed.

The first part of Jesus' answer is about what you must do to position yourself for admission into the final gathering of the saved. The person who posed the question rightly recognized that salvation is God's work. The passive voice of the verb "be saved" implies that one does not save oneself, but the redeeming action is done by God. However, as Jesus' response makes clear, one must engage in rigorous training in order to be in condition to accept the gift of being saved.

Jesus advises that one must "[s]trive to enter through the narrow gate." The verb *agōnizomai*, "strive," is used to describe athletic training (similarly, see 1 Cor 9:25). Just as an athlete must gradually build up strength through daily disciplined exercise, so spiritual fitness takes consistent effort and training. Jesus notes that many who attempt to enter will not be strong enough. The second reading from Hebrews also focuses on the discipline necessary to build up spiritual strength. Five times the author uses words derived from the Greek *paideuō* and *paideia*, which have to do with "discipline." The primary meaning is "instruction, training for responsible living."

The author makes an analogy between the training that a child receives from a parent and the guidance God provides us for deepening in the spiritual life. The Greek noun here means not so much punishment for wrongdoing as training for life. Some discipline consists in self-imposed, chosen actions that strengthen the spirit and enable one to follow the path of faithfulness. Other modes of life-shaping experiences are not purposely chosen, but how we deal with them forms us spiritually.

The author of Hebrews focuses on the latter kind of formation. He speaks of how God, like a loving parent, can help us to learn from the difficulties that befall us and can guide us in how to become stronger through them. In the author's worldview, everything that happens, both for good and for ill, is caused by God, so the writer suggests that God imposes trials as discipline.

His analogy of God as a loving parent, however, leads us also to think of God as never purposely inflicting suffering on us. The end result is that our spiritual "gymnastic" efforts (the verb *gymnazō* in v. 11 is a term for athletic training) lead to peace, joy, and right relation, with our drooping hands and weak knees healed and strengthened.

In the gospel Jesus speaks about what can happen to those who do not put any effort into "working out" spiritually. When the final moment comes, they will be on the outside pleading to get in, thinking that just having been present where Jesus was teaching would be enough. It is like someone who goes to the gym but only watches other people go through their paces. Such a one is not known in the company of athletes or prepared to make it to the finish line, "the narrow gate," and it will be too late then to start training. Jesus returns to the original question and, echoing the first reading from Isaiah, envisions masses of people from all directions who will be included among those saved. We may be surprised by who gets there first.

PRAYING WITH SCRIPTURE

1. Of what does your daily spiritual "workout" consist?

2. Ask the Divine Trainer to show you what needs strengthening.

3. How has God helped you grow stronger through difficult times?

EARTHY WISDOM

Twenty-Second Sunday in Ordinary Time

Readings: Sir 3:17-18, 20, 28-29;
Ps 68:4-5, 6-7, 10-11; Heb 12:18-19, 22-24a; Luke 14:1, 7-14

> *"Humble yourself the more, the greater you are,*
> *and you will find favor with God"* (Sir 3:18)

Every culture has its proverbs—pithy sayings that give wisdom about how to live well. The readings from both Sirach and the gospel pass on proverbial wisdom about the virtue of humility. This is earthy wisdom. The word *humility* comes from the Latin word *humilis*, which means literally "on the ground," deriving from *humus*, "earth." So when we are advised to humble ourselves, it is an invitation to be "grounded," to be attentive to our connectedness with Earth. This entails consciousness of our interconnectedness with all persons and all Earth's creatures and with God. As Ben Sira, who penned the book of Sirach, avers, in humbling oneself one finds favor with God. In other words, through humility we gain proper consciousness of our place in relation to God.

In the gospel, Jesus gives concrete examples of how one can go about growing in humility. He is at a dinner hosted by a leading Pharisee, and the invited guests are watching him closely. As the story progresses, there is growing hostility between Jesus and the Pharisees. Yet this is the third time he is said to be dining with them (see also Luke 7:36-50; 11:37-54).

One way in which Jesus models authentic humility is by not cutting off those whose theology and pastoral approach differ from his own. In Jesus' day, likes ate with likes. Eating together was a way to signify shared values. By dining with those who opposed him, he signaled that their shared common humanity forged a connection that superseded their differences.

Jesus first addresses the invited guests about choosing places at the table. The setting presumes that these are people with a certain measure of power and prestige. Banquets were occasions for people to enhance their social standing and Jesus describes how guests would compete for honor. The way to gain the most honor, he says, is actually to take the lowest place. Choosing to sit with those whose status would not enhance one's own personal honor could instead lead to growth in humility, that is, to engage in interactions with persons who are more *earthy* and to forge bonds with them. If such a person is then invited by the host to a higher position, he or she would be able to represent the perspectives of those at the other end of the table in the discussions and decisions that take place at the head.

Jesus then turns his attention to the host of the dinner and talks about how to formulate a guest list. From this angle, he again prods his hearers to break out of the strictures of likes eating with likes. The conversations at tables of the like-minded serve only to reinforce their own views, and the circle tightens as they reciprocate invitations to one another. Instead, Jesus proposes to the host, invite those unlike yourself, those with whom no one wants to associate. From a stance of humility, such a host recognizes the bond shared through common humanity that is stronger than differences in abilities or social positions.

It is easy to fall prey to false humility, pretending to take a lowly place in the hopes of receiving adulation and an invitation to come up higher. Or false humility can be manifest in persons whose self-esteem has never developed properly. True humility is grounded in earthy wisdom, a knowledge that all persons, no matter their circumstances, and all the created world share in an unbreakable interconnection of life given by God. We are equally loved and esteemed by the Holy One who desires the flourishing of all.

PRAYING WITH SCRIPTURE

1. Let Earth speak to you of the interconnectedness of all life and your place within the cosmos.

2. How does Jesus' practice of inviting those who were poor to join him speak to you?

3. What does today's gospel prompt us to consider regarding our gatherings at the eucharistic table?

CALCULATING THE COST

Twenty-Third Sunday in Ordinary Time

Readings: Wis 9:13-18b;
Ps 90:3-4, 5-6, 12-13, 14-17; Phlm 9-10, 12-17; Luke 14:25-33

"[F]irst sit down and calculate the cost" (Luke 14:28)

A few years ago we were privileged to host Jean Vanier and a companion from L'Arche at our school. There were huge crowds—it was standing room only, as people flocked to listen to this giant of a man share his saintly wisdom. All were enthralled with the way he spoke about the gospel and how he and his community tried to live it out. Anticipating an enthusiastic response, at the end of his remarks, Jean looked very seriously at the crowd, and advised that any who were thinking that they would like to take up the kind of ministry he had founded to be very sure that they could sustain a commitment for the long haul. He described in sober terms the difficulties and the sacrifices necessary to create inclusive, peaceful communities, where persons with and without physical and mental disabilities could live together in loving union.

A similar scene confronts us in today's gospel. Great crowds who were being healed and fed by Jesus were following him as he traveled. He addresses them in very sober terms about what it takes to stay with him for the whole way. He speaks about calculating the cost, not to dissuade any potential disciples, but rather to be sure that they are aware of what commitment to him demands, lest they be caught unaware. He names three of the greatest stumbling blocks: attachment to family, to possessions, and to life itself. None of these in themselves are wrong, but for disciples these attachments cannot take priority over attachment to Jesus.

The saying about hating one's own family members is jolting to our ears, as it was to Jesus' first followers. In Jesus' time, people did not conceive of themselves as individuals but derived their identity and social standing from their family, clan, village, and religious group. It would be unimaginable to cut oneself off from family; this would be tantamount to losing life itself.

Looking at other passages in the Gospel of Luke, we see that Jesus himself does not renounce his family. Unlike Mark (3:30-34), Luke (8:21) leaves open the possibility that Jesus' blood kin can also be disciples. In fact, Luke portrays Jesus' mother as one who faithfully hears the word of God and obeys; and in the story of Pentecost (Acts 1:14), Luke notes that Jesus' mother and siblings are among the disciples in the Upper Room. What Jesus asks, however, is that a disciple be willing to embrace as kin others who are not related by blood. Disciples must act as brother and sister toward those who are different, whether by physical ability or any other status marker. For some disciples, this new family will cause tension and even rupture in one's biological family. A disciple needs to be forewarned of this difficulty and be prepared to confront it. We see a concrete example in the second reading, in which Paul implores Philemon, the slave owner, to accept the slave Onesimus as a brother and an equal.

There is a curious twist in the gospel, as the parables Jesus tells would seem to advise building up one's resources in order to accomplish one's ends. The final verse takes us in exactly the opposite direction—calculating the cost of discipleship leads one to total divestment! In addition, we might note that although Luke envisions only male disciples in 14:26, elsewhere he clearly depicts women disciples (e.g., Mary Magdalene, Joanna, Susanna, and the Galilean women in Luke 8:1-3; 23:44-56; 24:1-12; Tabitha in Acts 9:36; Lydia in Acts 16; Prisca in Acts 18) whose attachment to Jesus superseded love of family, possessions, and life itself.

PRAYING WITH SCRIPTURE

1. Pray for the grace to let no other attachment take precedence over your commitment to follow Christ.

2. How has the Spirit empowered you to choose a path of costly discipleship?

3. When have you facilitated a costly choice as Paul did with Philemon and Onesimus?

THE GOD WHO SEEKS

Twenty-Fourth Sunday in Ordinary Time

Readings: Exod 32:7-11, 13-14;
Ps 51:3-4, 12-13, 17, 19; 1 Tim 1:12-17; Luke 15:1-32

"Or what woman having ten coins . . ." (Luke 15:8)

Some years ago in São Paulo, Brazil, a minister who worked with street children related how she was introducing them to Bible stories and helping them to reflect on them. One day she told the story of the prodigal son. She stopped at the point where the younger son decided to return home, and she asked if he would be able to go back home. One youngster spoke up. "It depends," he said. "On what?" she asked. "On whether there is a mother in the house. If so, then she will work on the father and get him to finally accept the son back."

This boy had rightly intuited the cultural dynamics of Jesus' day, which perhaps matched those of his own family. A father in a patriarchal culture whose son had so disgraced him would have rent his garments and declared that son no longer one of his own. We find a very different sort of father in the gospel, more like a mother who watches and waits and runs to meet the wayward son when he finally appears on the horizon. Such an image ruptures any patriarchal images of God and keeps us from literalizing the metaphor "Father."

Today's gospel presses further in offering a fuller set of images of the divine. God can also be likened to a shepherd (who could be either male or female), who diligently searches for a lost sheep. Jesus' first hearers would have understood the great lengths that shepherd went to, searching hither and yon for the lost one, and the great amount of energy it would take to hoist the heavy animal onto his shoulders and lug it back to the sheepfold. It is startling that instead of complaining, he is filled with joy! A footnote to the story: Some people worry about the ninety-nine left in the desert while the shepherd is off searching for the lost one. Jesus' original audience would have known that a flock that size would have had more than one shepherd, and the ninety-nine are not left untended. All are precious and are in the divine care.

Most often overlooked by homilists and biblical interpreters is the little parable in the middle of the trilogy. This parable mirrors the very same dynamics as the other two, this time proposing the image of a woman who searches intently for a lost coin. Just as a sheep and a son are so valuable that they must be sought out when lost and celebrated when found, so a drachma—enough to feed the family for a day. It is not a trivial bit of pocket change, nor is there any carelessness on the part of the woman. The point is that just as the shepherd goes to extraordinary lengths to find the lost sheep, so the woman uses precious lamp oil and searches unceasingly under stubborn cobblestones in the floor, until she finds where the errant coin has lodged. Shepherd, woman, and father are all equally good images for God, who expends great effort to procure the return of the lost and who hosts an exuberant celebration in their honor.

The trilogy of parables in today's gospel invites us to seek and retrieve the lost and overlooked female images of God. This enables a fuller experience of the divine, aids us in seeing women as images of God, and keeps us from idolatry, against which the first reading warns. Jesus himself invites us to stretch our imaginations, as he takes on the persona of Woman Wisdom in the opening verses of the gospel, where he is criticized for the company he keeps at table. Like Woman Wisdom (Prov 9:1-6), he has welcomed a scraggly array of all types to dine with him. We can stay outside and grumble, or we can enter into the party and allow ourselves to be surprised by the host.

PRAYING WITH SCRIPTURE

1. Pray with the image of the searching woman and ask God to reveal its meaning to you.

2. Let yourself be found and rejoiced over by God, and give thanks for this gift.

3. What diligent efforts are needed to search out and celebrate with lost images of God?

GRACE-FILLED COMPLEXITY

Twenty-Fifth Sunday in Ordinary Time

Readings: Amos 8:4-7;
Ps 113:1-2, 4-6, 7-8; 1 Tim 2:1-8; Luke 16:1-13

"What shall I do . . . ?" (Luke 16:3)

Things are not as simple as they used to be—or so it seems! Perhaps there never really was a time when issues were clear-cut and moral decisions were easy. In our time, technology allows choices never before possible. Decisions about medical choices, for example, particularly those involving beginning and ending of life, are more complex than ever before. In global economic systems the ramifications of our choices now go far beyond our local and immediate venues. How to understand complex systems and make good moral choices is a question that today's gospel can open up for us.

The parable in today's gospel is itself so complex that the only thing biblical scholars agree on is that it poses more questions than it answers, and no interpretation fully answers all of them. Questions such as these confront us: How can a dishonest steward be praised by his master? Who is the master? Jesus? The rich man? Is the parable about lost honor or lost income? What is the economic system presumed in the story? Does it concern usury? Or the steward's commission? What does "squandering" signify? Is the charge true or false? Who are the debtors? Is the master a sympathetic character or a villain? Is the steward someone to be emulated or is he a picaresque character designed to give us a chuckle in a comic story?

To complicate things further, it seems that the original parable of Jesus ends at verse 8a, and verses 8b to 13 are more like homily notes of early interpreters. These verses are stitched together by catchwords offering four different interpretations around the theme of the right use of money, none of which really captures the dynamics of the parable proper.

One possibility for this Sunday is not to try to settle the interpretation of the gospel parable but to look instead at the underlying values and attitudes that the readings propose, which orient us toward what we must do in order to be able to make good moral decisions in complex situations. In the first reading, the situation seems straightforward: the dishonest merchants cannot wait for the Sabbath to be over so they can return to cheating the poor.

As with Amos, our first important step is to cultivate the ability to see from the perspective of those made poor and to be outraged, as he was, about economic practices that feed greed and "trample upon the needy." Once one sees these practices, it is then important to do whatever is possible to counter them. Publicly raising one's voice, as did Amos when telling the truth about the unjust practices, is one important response. Another is to observe Sabbath days, when rest and communal and contemplative prayer can help communities of faith to cultivate eyes that see what is needed for the common good. A Sabbath rest from buying and selling also provides a hiatus from exploitation of the poor and cultivates reliance on providence.

The letter to Timothy reminds us of the importance of praying for all those in authority, so that they will be persons of wisdom, able to lead in such a way that all can enjoy a dignified and tranquil life. From the gospel, we can see that a time of crisis is an opportunity to assess one's own or a community's strengths and weaknesses while weighing different possibilities for the future. Cultivating relationships, as did the steward, is essential. When all these values and practices are put together, then a creative solution for the common good emerges, and decisive action can be taken.

PRAYING WITH SCRIPTURE

1. How does Sabbath rest enable you to see more clearly and allow the Spirit to guide you in complex decisions?

2. Pray for those in authority in the various arenas of your life.

3. How do you cultivate an ear for the voices of those made poor?

THE BRIDGEABLE CHASM

Twenty-Sixth Sunday in Ordinary Time

Readings: Amos 6:1a, 4-7;
Ps 146:7, 8-9, 9-10; 1 Tim 6:11-16; Luke 16:19-31

"[B]etween us and you a great chasm is established" (Luke 16:26)

Stories of the ongoing misery in Haiti in the aftermath of a devastating earthquake continue to appear in our news. *The New York Times* (on August 9, 2010) told the story of Alourds Grandoit, age seventy, who had lost ten family members when her house collapsed on them. Left with next to nothing, a plastic barrel full of clothing, toiletries, and food was wending its way to her from her cousin, Gislaine Vieux, in Queens, New York. Gislaine had left Haiti forty-one years ago in search of work in the United States to be able to help support her family in Haiti. For thirty years her income from her hospital job has helped sustain her struggling relatives. Now, she and her husband are also helping coordinate their parish's response of monetary aid and relief missions to her homeland.

The gap between Gislaine's modest home in Queens and the unspeakable conditions in which many live in Port-au-Prince might at first appear unbridgeable, but ties of family and loving commitment to one another forge bonds unbroken by geographical and socioeconomic distance. By contrast, in today's gospel Jesus tells a story of a rich man who steps over a destitute brother who is lying right at his doorstep. The rich man pays no attention to the poor man, Lazarus, until he needs something from him. From his tormented place in the afterlife, the rich man wants Lazarus to bring him the relief of cool water. When Abraham replies that this is impossible, then the rich man asks Abraham to send Lazarus to warn his brothers.

The rich man was not able during his earthly life, nor afterward, to perceive the poor man as one of his brothers, even when he sees Lazarus intimately embraced (literally, "in his bosom"; v. 23 in Greek) as one of Abraham's own. The rich man calls Abraham his own father in order to claim what he thinks is his privileged inheritance. He has not shared his wealth as Abraham did when he was wealthy (Gen 24:35), nor does he claim the rest of Abraham's children as his brothers and sisters. He sees Lazarus only as his servant and messenger.

Abraham does not grant the rich man either request. The vast differences between him and Lazarus could have been bridged during the rich man's lifetime, but he chose not to respond to his brother. Now the consequences of those repeated choices cannot be reversed. He had everything he needed from Moses and the prophets to know what to do. So do his rich brothers. It is not enough to claim kinship with Abraham.

As John the Baptist had warned the crowds who came to be baptized, it is also necessary to "[p]roduce good fruits as evidence of your repentance" (Luke 3:8, NABRE). Jesus' practice of recognizing people who were marginalized as sisters and brothers, children of Abraham, like the woman bent double for eighteen years (Luke 13:16) and Zacchaeus, the tax collector (Luke 19:9), also shows the way. Ironically, the rich man asks for Lazarus to "warn" his brothers, using the verb *diamartyromai*, one that occurs nine times in the Acts of the Apostles to refer to "bearing witness" to the risen Jesus. Even testimony about the risen Jesus will not turn the hearts of the rich brothers.

Moses, the prophets, and Jesus have given us all we need to know in order to bridge the chasm between rich and poor in this life. We begin by recognizing those made poor not as an abstraction but as real persons who have names, most of whom are women and children, who are sister and brother to us, and to whom we are bound in covenantal love. From there, the gap is bridgeable.

PRAYING WITH SCRIPTURE

1. Ask the help of the risen Jesus to see and to love each person as sister and brother.

2. Pray for the grace to act in ways that help bridge the chasm between rich and poor.

3. Ask Holy Wisdom to guide you in how to respond to the feminization of poverty.

THE TIMELY VISION

Twenty-Seventh Sunday in Ordinary Time

Readings: Hab 1:2-3; 2:2-4;
Ps 95:1-2, 6-7, 8-9; 2 Tim 1:6-8, 13-14; Luke 17:5-10

"Write down the vision clearly" (Hab 2:2)

The lament of the prophet Habakkuk, as he decries the violence, strife, and clamorous discord in his day, seems to have a timelessness to it. During the hot summer, several US cities saw a spike in gun violence and senseless deaths. Public discourse has grown more rancorous as marchers proclaim competing visions for what would make for a peaceable world.

Habakkuk wants God to intervene and put an end to the distress of his time. God's answer to Habakkuk is an order to write down the vision clearly upon tablets so that everyone can read it readily. The prophet is reminded that although it seems long in coming, the vision of God's peaceable reign will surely be fulfilled. He must be patient and stay faithful.

The divine directive to Habakkuk is an excellent reminder to us that no transformative change ever comes without being grounded in the vision of God's peaceable reign. It is not enough, however, to wait patiently and persistently keep the vision alive in one's own mind and heart. God directs the prophet to write down the vision, not only to keep it before his own eyes as a way to bolster his own flagging hope, but also to publicize it so that it boosts communal faith and committed action.

It is precisely when things seem at their worst that the prophet is called to articulate the vision. In the struggle for civil rights in the United States, it was when the backlash against Martin Luther King Jr.'s vision for an end to racism was most intense that he publicly proclaimed the dream of equality and freedom for all. Likewise, it is from prison, where Paul is suffering great hardship, that he writes the vision for Timothy, reminding him that God has given him the power of love, self-control, and strength. By stirring this gift into flame, he can overcome any fear or cowardice in giving his testimony to the gospel.

Not unlike Habakkuk, the disciples in today's gospel want Jesus to fix things by giving them more faith. Jesus reassures them that they already have faith enough to transform what seems utterly immovable. A mulberry tree has a deep and extensive root system and is extremely difficult to up-root and replant. It is an apt image for deep-rooted systems of injustice and violence. A mustard seed, by contrast, is tiny, but spreads like wildfire, and is also nearly impossible to eradicate. Disciples who feel puny in the face of massive systems of injustice have all they need to do the transformative work toward fulfillment of Jesus' vision of the reign of God. Jesus encourages them by saying not only that they have all the faith they need but also that it is by their persistent, day-in, day-out service that the transformation of seemingly intractable systems comes about. Moreover, just as fieldwork and table service were simply what was required of a slave in Jesus' time, so faithful service on behalf of the gospel is what is expected of disciples. One way in which the analogy limps, however, is that discipleship is a freely chosen service, not an imposed servility embedded in an unjust system.

The final verse of today's gospel does not assert that faithful servants are "unprofitable" (NABRE), "worthless" (NRSV), or "useless" (NJB), as some translations render the Greek *achreioi*. Rather, the word literally means that they are "without need." Proclaiming the empowering vision of God's reign and rendering faithful service to bring it about satisfies every want and need of disciples.

PRAYING WITH SCRIPTURE

1. What is your vision of God's peaceable reign? Write it down.

2. Pray with gratitude for the sufficiency of your mustard seed-sized faith.

3. Pray for the gift of self-emptying so as to be "without need."

SAVING GRATITUDE

Twenty-Eighth Sunday in Ordinary Time

Readings:
2 Kgs 5:14-17; Ps 98:1, 2-3, 3-4; 2 Tim 2:8-13; Luke 17:11-19

"And one of them, realizing he had been healed,
returned, glorifying God in a loud voice" (Luke 17:15)

One of our sisters, as she approached her golden jubilee, was repeatedly heard to say, "I have all I need." She had always lived very simply, and her stance of radical gratitude was infectious as she invited all whom she encountered to join her in this thankful space.

The first reading and the gospel today tell stories of two different men afflicted with leprosy. One was a mighty warrior, commander of the army of the king of Aram. The other is huddled with a pitiful group of nine others likewise afflicted. The first, called Naaman, has easy access to the king. The one in the gospel is nameless and is ostracized by all, keeping his distance even from Jesus. Both are foreigners who nonetheless are healed by Israel's prophets, Elisha and Jesus. Both praise the God of Israel for their transformation.

In the gospel account, the focus is on the way the one healed man turns around and loudly glorifies God, falling at Jesus' feet, thanking him. It is a dramatic enactment of the stance of saving gratitude that divine gifts evoke. Jesus affirms the man's response and tells him to go, that his faith has saved him. Luke does not elaborate what was the man's inner disposition before he was healed. Was he filled with self-pity? Was he consumed with longing for well-being? Was he bitter or despairing over his deteriorating physical state?

At the realization of his healing, the man turned around, perhaps not only physically but interiorly as well. When he lets gratitude for all God has given him consume him, he turns around from any other cancers that eat at his spirit. Jesus affirms that this kind of faith, rooted in thankfulness, is the healing, saving power (the Greek verb *sōzein* connotes both "heal" and "save") that enables him to go forward as a changed person, both in body and spirit.

In the first reading, Naaman has a much more difficult time accepting the full transformation offered to him. In the verses leading up to today's Lectionary selection, Naaman takes huge amounts of silver, gold, and clothing, along with a letter from his king, when he approaches the king of Israel to ask for healing from the foreign prophet. He then goes to Elisha's house with horses, chariots, and all his retinue.

Elisha sends out a messenger, who directs Naaman to wash seven times in the Jordan River. Naaman is furious, declaring, "I thought that he would surely come out to me and stand there to call on the name of the LORD his God, and would move his hand over the place, and thus cure the leprous spot" (2 Kgs 5:11, NABRE). Because of his high position, Naaman feels entitled to special, personal attention. He is used to giving commands and has a fixed idea of how the healing should be done. And although he has crossed over into Israelite territory, he has no regard for their life-giving water. He insists that the rivers in his own land are better than the Jordan. After he departs in a rage, his servants persuade him to go back and immerse himself in the Jordan.

Naaman struggles mightily to turn away from his stance of entitlement, from his attempts to buy healing, and his efforts to direct the manner in which it should occur. After his healing, Naaman still tries to pay for it, but Elisha will take nothing from him. All that God or Jesus desires in return is a heart shaped by saving gratitude for freely given grace that has the power to heal both the inner and outer self.

PRAYING WITH SCRIPTURE

1. Pray to be filled with gratitude, which displaces greed and entitlement.

2. How is gratitude to God a saving grace that is different from an enslaving stance of groveling dependence?

3. How can your stance of fundamental gratitude be a transforming power in the cosmos?

PERSISTENT PURSUIT OF JUSTICE

Twenty-Ninth Sunday in Ordinary Time

Readings: Exod 17:8-13;
Ps 121:1-2, 3-4, 5-6, 7-8; 2 Tim 3:14–4:2; Luke 18:1-8

"[B]e persistent whether it is convenient or inconvenient" (2 Tim 4:2)

For the past sixty-five years, Frances Crowe, now age ninety-one, has been protesting war and advocating for peace, human rights, and environmental justice. She has been arrested and imprisoned for leading public demonstrations more times than she can remember. This diminutive widow never tires of her persistent pursuit of justice. She seems the very embodiment of the widow in today's gospel.

Luke has framed the parable with introductory and concluding verses that were likely not part of the original parable Jesus told (preserved in vv. 2-5). The parable begins with the introduction of two characters: a judge who twice declares he has no fear of God and no respect for any human being; and a widow who comes to him over and over and over, day after day after day, insisting that justice be done. The imperfect tense of the verbs indicates repeated action; she comes again and again and won't give up until she gets a just verdict.

We can picture her coming back to the courtroom day after day, raising her voice in protest, calling out to the judge, telling him he might as well listen to her today, because if not, she'll be back tomorrow. She sees people with influence and money being attended to, while her only recourse is her voice and her presence. She breaks the stereotype of how widows are generally regarded.

Throughout the Hebrew Scriptures there is a repeated admonition to care for widows, along with orphans and strangers, the most vulnerable people in the society (e.g., Deut 24:17-21). This widow should be cared for by her nearest male relative, and it is he who should be pleading her case before the judge. Instead, the widow intrepidly enters into space usually reserved for males and will not give up until justice is accomplished.

The judge is impervious. He continues to ignore her until he can no longer stand her insistent protests. He has not been changed; he still insists he has no fear of God or respect for persons, but he finally relents because he is afraid she will haul off and give him a black eye! The verb *hypōpiazein* in verse 5 is often translated metaphorically as "wear me out," but it is a boxing term that literally means "to strike under the eye" (see also 1 Cor 9:27). It is a hilarious image: a supposedly powerful judge cowering in front of a seemingly powerless little widow.

The humorous vignette, however, conveys a very serious message: it is through persistence and tireless actions of nonviolent confrontation that justice is attained. More often than not, this happens through the repeated actions of seemingly inconsequential people, who never give up. In a patriarchal world, we are inclined to look to the powerful male figure to be the God-like character. But in this parable it is the widow who embodies the divine insistence on justice and who most resembles Jesus' manner of tirelessly preaching and acting to bring it about.

Persistent prayer goes hand in hand with persistent action for justice. In order to sustain the constant struggle for peace, the heart and mind must be continually transformed by the One who is our source of peace. The first reading reminds us that this is not a solitary effort. Like Moses, we need companions to hold up our arms when we grow weary, and like Frances Crowe, we need to engage other faithful friends in our persistent actions for justice. Fearless, because she has nothing to lose, she vows, "as long as I have energy, I'm going to keep at it" (quoted in David Abel, "A Protester for the Ages," *Boston Globe* [September 13, 2010]).

PRAYING WITH SCRIPTURE

1. How does your faithfulness to prayer embolden you for persistent actions for justice?

2. Who holds you up when you become weary? Whom do you hold up?

3. How do you use the power of your voice and your presence in advocating for justice?

INCOMPARABLE MERCY

Thirtieth Sunday in Ordinary Time

Readings: Sir 35:12-14, 16-18;
Ps 34:2-3, 17-18, 19, 23; 2 Tim 4:6-8, 16-18; Luke 18:9-14

"O God, be merciful to me a sinner" (Luke 18:13)

"Comparisons are odious," wrote John Lydgate in his poem "Horse, Goose, and Sheep," which dates to the mid-fifteenth century. In the poem, the animals debate which one is more useful to human beings. The poem creatively exposes how boastful comparisons fuel attitudes of superiority and disdain for others. In much the same way, Jesus uses parables, like the one in today's gospel, to help his listeners identify and change behavior in themselves that is harmful.

Two characters, a Pharisee and a tax collector, go up to the temple to pray. Jesus' original audience would have instinctively compared them, thinking the first to be admirable, and the latter despicable. Pharisees were known for their piety. This particular one fasts and tithes above and beyond what is required. Surely these actions indicate that he is righteous, that is, in right relation with God, other human beings, and the whole of creation. The Pharisee's prayer, however, indicates otherwise. The entire prayer directs attention to himself and his accomplishments: "I thank you . . . I am not like . . . I fast . . . I give." He thanks God, not for the gifts he has been given, but for not being like all the rest of humanity, which he sees as rapacious, unjust, and adulterous. His comparisons make him haughty, and disconnected from others. Moreover, he appears to have no need of God. If he were to direct his gaze at God, he might arrive at a different kind of comparison. He might see how poorly he embodies divine compassion and connectedness to all other beings.

The tax collector, in contrast, beats his breast and prays simply, "O God, be merciful to me a sinner." Focusing on God, he prays for openness to divine mercy, which has the power to transform his sinfulness.

It is likely that he finds himself in this degraded position of collecting taxes because there are no alternatives. One would only stoop to such a job when no other work could be found. Tax collectors were low-level functionaries with no bargaining power. If they extorted money beyond what was their due, it was out of desperation, to keep starvation at bay. Should the tax collector try to repent, there would be no way to repay the many passersby from whom he exacted extra money, so as he prays he offers no vow to make restitution. All he can hope for is God's merciful forgiveness.

The end of the parable is startling: it is the tax collector who is in right relation. He has sinned, but he knows and acknowledges it. He is acutely aware of his utter dependence on God. He does not compare himself to others but seeks connectedness to them, through their common bond of reliance on God's mercy.

The parable seems to invite comparison of the two characters, and we are wont to side with the tax collector. In the very act of making comparisons that reflect unfavorably on the Pharisee, however, we may find ourselves caught up in the very judgmental thinking we despise in him. In truth, there is something of the Pharisee in us, as we so easily make comparisons, exalting ourselves by humiliating others. There is also something of the tax collector in us, who humbly recognizes his own weaknesses while opening himself to the Source of all mercy. The parable invites us to leave aside all odious comparisons and to seek oneness with the incomparably Merciful One. From this stance comes right relation with all.

PRAYING WITH SCRIPTURE

1. Try to leave out "I" the next time you pray.

2. Pray with gratitude for the mercy you have received and let yourself be transformed by it.

3. Pray to let go of any tendencies to compare yourself to others.

OUT ON A LIMB

Thirty-First Sunday in Ordinary Time

Readings: Wis 11:22–12:2;
Ps 145:1-2, 8-9, 10-11, 13, 14; 2 Thess 1:11–2:2; Luke 19:1-10

"For the Son of Man has come to seek and to save what was lost" (Luke 19:10)

Jesus was accustomed to going out on a limb for people who were poor, sick, possessed by demons, or marginalized. He deliberately sought out such people. So when Jesus got to Jericho, with its luxurious villas of the rich, he did not even plan to stop there (Luke 19:1). The elite gravitated there because it was balmy all year-round. Only twenty-three miles from Jerusalem, which has an elevation of 2,700 feet, Jericho lies 770 feet below sea level—the lowest city on Earth. Moreover, the Dead Sea lies only ten miles to the south, with its spas and healing waters laden with salts and minerals. With its perennial spring, Jericho is an oasis in the desert, dotted with palm trees and producing luscious fruit all year-round. The people who could afford to live or vacation there were not the sort who were looking for what Jesus had to offer.

In addition, Jesus may have wanted to move quickly past Jericho because the Herodians, who wanted to kill him (13:31), had winter palaces there. Luke notes that Herod (Antipas) had long had a desire to see Jesus (9:9), a desire that is finally fulfilled after Jesus' arrest (23:8). In today's gospel, Zacchaeus also desires to see Jesus, and goes to extraordinary lengths to do so.

Zacchaeus has become rich himself, but through a most ignoble profession. Hated by his own people as a quisling of Rome, he would also have been despised for lining his own pockets with money extorted in his work. No one would take the job of tax collector unless he was desperate. Rare would be one who could work the system to make himself as rich as Zacchaeus. One wonders what it had cost him to get to become chief tax collector. What values had he compromised? What people had he defrauded? What relationships had been sacrificed?

In an instant, Zacchaeus risks the social stature he has so carefully built up. Small in physical stature, he acts in a most undignified way, racing ahead of the crowd, and climbing a tree! When Jesus sees how far out on a limb Zacchaeus has gone, he does the same. Calling him down, Jesus announces he must stay at Zacchaeus's house. Grumbling and criticism of Jesus for staying with a sinner immediately follow. But the risk Jesus takes for Zacchaeus is worth it.

Like Martha, who received (*hypedexato*) Jesus into her home (10:38), and like Mary Magdalene, whose discipleship was expressed in financial service (8:3), so Zacchaeus receives (*hypedexato*) Jesus with joy, opening his heart and his wallet in generous outreach. Zacchaeus declares that half his possessions will go to the poor, and any ill-gotten money he will repay four times over. In addition to his dignity and reputation, Zacchaeus now risks his financial security and his social standing among his rich cohorts. The gospel is not specific about the ways in which Zacchaeus felt lost, nor what prompted him to look to Jesus to be found. Nonetheless, Jesus perceives Zacchaeus's need and leaves with him the saving grace to negotiate the challenges ahead.

Jesus does not ask Zacchaeus to leave behind his profession nor to give away the rest of his possessions. Rather, he meets him in the place of his seeking and opens up a saving way forward within his circumstances. One wonders what will be the cost to Zacchaeus to live out of this saving grace. Will he be ostracized by the Jericho elites? Will he follow Jesus out onto the final limb, the tree of the cross? Will his life, like that of Jesus, seed new shoots of hope and life? Will ours?

PRAYING WITH SCRIPTURE

1. Pray with gratitude for the times that Jesus has gone out on a limb for you.

2. How does Jesus empower you to take risks for the sake of the gospel?

3. Join the chorus of all the saints who praise God for the gift of salvation.

ANGELIC LEGACY

Thirty-Second Sunday in Ordinary Time

Readings: 2 Macc 7:1-2, 9-14;
Ps 17:1, 5-6, 8, 15; 2 Thess 2:16-35; Luke 20:27-38

"They can no longer die, for they are like angels;
and they are the children of God" (Luke 20:36)

There is within the human spirit an indomitable will to live—not only our earthly life but also beyond it. Few share the perspective of the artist Andy Warhol: "I never understood why when you died, you didn't just vanish. Everything could just keep going on the way it was only you just wouldn't be there. I always thought I'd like my own tombstone to be blank. No epitaph, and no name."

Most people want to be remembered for having made a difference in the world during their earthly sojourn. Sometimes we muse about what we would want on our tombstone. For what do we most want to be remembered? For people in Jesus' day, it was important to leave their mark in the world through the children they left behind. Some, like the Sadducees, did not believe in any other form of life beyond the grave.

The notion of resurrected life only began to emerge some two hundred years before Jesus. Ideas varied about what it would be like. In the first reading today, we see the belief expressed that only the just would be raised, not the wicked. In other texts, we find the notion that both would be raised, the former for eternal reward, the latter for everlasting punishment (Matt 25:46).

In the gospel today, some Sadducees pose to Jesus what looks like a preposterous question. As usual, they are antagonistic toward Jesus and their question is meant to show the impossibility of resurrection, a belief Jesus espoused (see Luke 14:14). They try to show that Jesus' belief is at odds with the law of Moses. They cite the levirate law (Deut 25:5-6), whose intent was to insure that a man's name not be blotted out of Israel. Instead, the Sadducees frame the question in terms of the men's possession of the woman in the afterlife.

Jesus' response undoes their misperceptions by affirming that there will be no patriarchal marital arrangements in the afterlife. There will be no need to ensure one's legacy through the children one leaves behind. Rather, one continues to live as God's child, no longer haunted by the shadow of death. Using their own exegetical tools, Jesus shows the Sadducees that Moses himself can be read as affirming that life continues beyond the grave. We can hear as well, in Jesus' response, God's desire for an end to any abuse of women. As beloved daughters of God, they are no longer passed on from man to man.

Feeding our curiosity about what resurrected life will be like, Jesus drops one small hint: "they are like angels," or heavenly messengers (*angelos* in Greek means "messenger"). In Luke's gospel angels appear at the most critical moments. Their function is to interpret puzzling and disturbing events through divine eyes. Gabriel announces to Zechariah and to Mary God's ability to bring forth life and blessing in the most impossible of circumstances. At the transfiguration, two heavenly messengers, Moses and Elijah, interpret Jesus' impending death as the new exodus (the Greek word *exodos* means both "departure" and "death") to liberated life (Luke 9:31). At the empty tomb, two angelic figures (24:4-7) convey a message of hope in the most terrible moment. Angelic life, as Luke portrays it, consists in being a messenger of hope in the most awful of circumstances. It is the refusal already in this life to allow evil to triumph; it is not simply delayed reward in the beyond. It is, as Maya Angelou wrote of the "dreams and the hopes of the slave" in her poem "Still I Rise": "You may shoot me with your words/You may cut me with your eyes/You may kill me with your hatefulness/But still, like air, I'll rise."

PRAYING WITH SCRIPTURE

1. How does belief in resurrection make you a messenger of hope in the present?

2. How are you already writing your own tombstone?

3. Contemplate the God of the living, to whom all are alive.

FEARLESS TESTIMONY

Thirty-Third Sunday in Ordinary Time

Readings:
Mal 3:19-20a; Ps 98:5-6, 7-8, 9; 2 Thess 3:7-12; Luke 21:5-19

"[D]o not be terrified . . . I myself shall give you a wisdom in speaking"
(Luke 21:9, 15)

I live in Chicago, a city that boasts of its exquisite architecture, and it is easy for me to imagine the admiration of the people in today's gospel for the monumental temple in Jerusalem. Although they weren't snapping photos and posing in front of skyscrapers, as contemporary tourists do, they seem to have been caught up in the same wonder and awe that is evoked by grand buildings. People marvel at the engineering genius of the construction. In the case of temples and cathedrals, their beauty and grandeur lift the mind and heart and help human beings feel connected to the divine.

The reverie of the onlookers in today's gospel is broken suddenly by Jesus' declaration that not one stone would be left upon another. As a Jewish reformer, Jesus frequently spoke and acted in ways that called into question religious structures, both external and internal, that impeded right relationship with God and one another. But for any Jew, the destruction of the temple by Roman imperial forces would provoke a severe crisis. Everything would have to be resignified. The temple symbolized their connection with God and with their fellow believers. And it was in the temple that the sacrificial cult was exercised in obedience to the commands of the Torah.

Luke's gospel, of course, was written some fifteen years after the temple had been razed. We can imagine the struggles of the Jewish Christian members of the Lukan community who had to redefine their Jewishness, not only in the absence of their temple, but also as members of a mixed community of Gentile and Jewish followers of Jesus. The Gentile members also had to reconstruct their internal architecture when they took on a Christian identity.

In today's gospel, there is a progression, as the discussion moves from the destruction of the temple to cataclysmic happenings that wreak destruction on the earth and among peoples and, finally, to threats against one's life. It envisions crises on every level, moving toward an apocalyptic end time. Jesus' audience does not ask if such will happen. Rather, they ask when it will come about and if they will have advance warning. Jesus never answers those questions. Instead, he directs his listeners how to respond to these crises. If they are following him, then they too will say and do things that threaten some of the political and religious structures of their day. Any who claim his name will surely experience the same kind of fury that was directed at him for doing such things.

Jesus does not leave his disciples defenseless in such times of crisis. First of all, he reminds his followers not to follow after anyone else; their attention must remain steadfastly on him. When their focus is on him and not on their tribulations, they are able to stand fearless. He speaks the same words that Gabriel spoke to Zechariah and Mary when their worlds were being turned upside down: "Do not be afraid" (Luke 1:13, 30, NABRE).

When disciples are seized and persecuted and handed over to the authorities because of Jesus' name, these are times to testify to the power of God. Jesus explains that the testimony is not a speech that one composes ahead of time. The preparation consists in persevering in a life of faithfulness and trust in the One who provoked crises by his manner of life. It is he, who is himself the temple (to borrow from Johannine theology), who will give the necessary wisdom for speech and action in the critical moment.

PRAYING WITH SCRIPTURE

1. How does keeping our focus on Jesus enable us to be fearless in times of crises?

2. When have you experienced the power of Christ speaking through you?

3. What support structures enable you to persevere?

ROYAL FORGIVENESS

The Solemnity of Christ the King

Readings: 2 Sam 5:1-3;
Ps 122:1-2, 3-4, 4-5; Col 1:12-20; Luke 23:35-43

"Jesus, remember me when you come into your kingdom" (Luke 23:42)

In December 1997, Las Abejas, a group of forty-eight indigenous communities whose name means "the bees," came to the world's attention when forty-five of their members, mostly women and children, were murdered. They were killed by paramilitary troops while they were fasting and praying for peace in their rough-hewn wooden chapel in the village of Acteal, Mexico. Las Abejas come from the highlands of Chiapas, in the southernmost part of Mexico. They call themselves Las Abejas because they see themselves as a community of equal worker bees, striving together for peace, all serving the queen bee, which is the reign of God. No person other than Jesus and his kingdom can be the center of their hive of activity.

Several years after the massacre, a group of our students and professors was privileged to meet with their community. We asked if they were not tempted to abandon their commitment to nonviolence after they had lost so many of their mothers and sisters and brothers.

Without hesitation, they replied that they must continue to forgive their enemies and pray for their persecutors because that is what Jesus did. It is a powerful appropriation of the example of Christ given to us in today's gospel.

Some people in Jesus' day were looking for a king like David, who would reassert Israel's independence, rid the land of the Romans, and make wise decisions for the people.

There were advantages to monarchical rule: one man invested with authority could carry the weight of governance and make decisions on behalf of the people. But there were also disadvantages. What if the ruler did not have foremost the peoples' best interest? What if his judgment was impaired by greed and hunger for power? What voice did the common folk have in decisions that affected their lives? What chance was there that women's perspectives would be heard?

When Jesus appeared, proclaiming God's kingdom, he offered an antidote to imperial ways. He criticized the way the "kings of the Gentiles" lorded their power over their people and demanded recognition for their benefaction.

By contrast, he urged the leaders among his followers to be the servants of all (Luke 22:25-26), a manner of life he modeled for them, as he took up his itinerant mission with people at the lowest rungs of society. Unlike an offended monarch who imposes harsh punishments for infractions, he instead exercised power through forgiveness and compassion when there were transgressions.

Today's gospel paints in stark contrast the power of imperial Rome, which brooks no challenges to its rule, and the "kingly" ways of Jesus that rest on forgiveness and love. Even as it appears that the former may win out, the gospel makes it utterly clear that Jesus' merciful rule cannot be extinguished by death.

Even as he is mocked and taunted in his dying moments, Jesus continues to exercise the power of forgiveness both toward his executioners (23:34) and toward one of the criminals who acknowledges his form of power and asks to be included in his realm.

Followers of Christ the King find themselves challenged to form communities of "worker bees," where the only royal figure is Jesus, where the only kingdom is God's, and where the power of forgiveness reigns supreme.

PRAYING WITH SCRIPTURE

1. Ask Christ to let the power of forgiveness rule your heart.

2. How is the power of forgiveness exercised in community?

3. How is Christ inviting you to be a servant-leader?